MIKE BARTLETT

Mike Bartlett is a multi-award-winning playwright and screenwriter whose most recent plays include a new version of *Vassa* by Maxim Gorky (Almeida Theatre); *Snowflake* (Old Fire Station/Kiln Theatre); *Albion* (Almeida Theatre); *Wild* (Hampstead Theatre); *Game* (Almeida Theatre); *King Charles III* (Almeida Theatre/West End/Broadway; Critics' Circle Award for Best New Play, Olivier Award for Best New Play, Tony Nomination for Best Play); *An Intervention* (Paines Plough/ Watford Palace Theatre); *Bull* (Sheffield Theatres/Off-Broadway; TMA Best New Play Award, Olivier Award for Outstanding Achievement in an Affiliate Theatre); *Medea* (Glasgow Citizens/ Headlong); *Chariots of Fire* (based on the film; Hampstead/West End); *13* (National Theatre); *Love, Love, Love* (Paines Plough/ Plymouth Drum/Royal Court Theatre; TMA Best New Play Award); *Earthquakes in London* (Headlong/National Theatre); *Cock* (Royal Court/Off-Broadway, Olivier Award for Outstanding Achievement in an Affiliate Theatre); *Artefacts* (nabokov/Bush Theatre); *Contractions* and *My Child* (Royal Court).

Bartlett has also written several plays for radio, winning the Writers' Guild Tinniswood and Imison Prizes for *Not Talking*. He has received BAFTA nominations for his television series *The Town* and *Doctor Foster*, for which Bartlett won Outstanding Newcomer for British Television Writing at the British Screenwriters' Awards 2016. Bartlett's adaptation of his play *King Charles III* aired on BBC television in 2017.

Mike Bartlett

ALBION

NICK HERN BOOKS

London

www.nickhernbooks.co.uk

A Nick Hern Book

Albion first published in Great Britain in 2017 as a paperback original by Nick Hern Books Limited, The Glasshouse, 49a Goldhawk Road, London W12 8QP

Reprinted in this revised edition 2020

Albion copyright © 2017, 2020 Mike Bartlett

Mike Bartlett has asserted his right to be identified as the author of this work

Cover design by Conductor for the Almeida Theatre

Designed and typeset by Nick Hern Books, London
Printed in Great Britain by Mimeo Ltd, Huntingdon, Cambridgeshire PE29 6XX

A CIP catalogue record for this book is available from the British Library

ISBN 978 1 84842 715 0

Albion was first performed at the Almeida Theatre, London, on 17 October 2017 (previews from 10 October), with the following cast:

EDWARD	Nigel Betts
KRYSTYNA	Edyta Budnik
WEATHERBURY/JAMES	Wil Coban
MATTHEW	Christopher Fairbank
AUDREY WALTERS	Victoria Hamilton
ZARA	Charlotte Hope
CHERYL	Margot Leicester
ANNA	Vinette Robinson
PAUL WALTERS	Nicholas Rowe
KATHERINE SANCHEZ	Helen Schlesinger
GABRIEL	Luke Thallon

Direction	Rupert Goold
Design	Miriam Buether
Lighting	Neil Austin
Sound	Gregory Clark
Movement Director	Rebecca Frecknall
Associate Movement Director	Gemma Payne
Casting	Amy Ball
Casting Assistant	Arthur Carrington
Resident Director	Tom Brennan
Costume Supervision	Anna Josephs
Dialect Coach	Charmian Hoare

The production was revived at the Almeida on 1 February 2020, with the following changes to the cast:

ANNA	Angel Coulby
ZARA	Daisy Edgar-Jones
GABRIEL	Dónal Finn
MATTHEW	Geoffrey Freshwater

Characters

AUDREY WALTERS, *fifties*
PAUL WALTERS, *her second husband, early sixties*
ZARA, *her daughter, early twenties*
ANNA, *her son's partner, thirties*
KATHERINE SANCHEZ, *her friend, fifties*
EDWARD, *a neighbour, mid-fifties*
KRYSTYNA, *a cleaner, early twenties*
CHERYL, *a cleaner, late sixties*
MATTHEW, *Cheryl's husband, a gardener, late sixties*
GABRIEL, *a neighbour, nineteen*

WEATHERBURY
JAMES
STANLEY

This text went to press before the end of rehearsals and so may differ slightly from the play as performed.

Prologue

Elgar plays.

'The Spirit of England Op.80 No. 3 – For The Fallen.'

WEATHERBURY, *an army captain, returns to his garden, Albion, after service in the First World War.*

He walks onto the empty patch of earth. It reminds him of the battlefield.

He looks around, then drinks out of his canteen.

He's alone.

He crouches down. Takes a handful of soil. Lets it run through his fingers.

Blackout.

Music continues...

ACT ONE

Late February.

Albion is a garden, now mostly left to ruin, attached to a house in Oxfordshire. There are many 'rooms' in the garden, but the play is set in the Red Garden.

Music fades…

The garden has been left to ruin for many years. The outline of the beds is still there with bricks, and the weeds have now been cleared, but there are few plants. An oak tree stands in the corner.

MATTHEW, *the gardener, enters with his wife* CHERYL, *mid-conversation.*

MATTHEW	I'm saying be more careful is all! I don't see how you could have got confused.
CHERYL	They're right next to each other.
MATTHEW	They're different colours.
CHERYL	They should make the hole a different size.
	A moment.
MATTHEW	You called the RAC.
CHERYL	I did. Took forty minutes. Not so bad. It was a man with an accent who came.
MATTHEW	What accent?
CHERYL	I don't know.
MATTHEW	– we talking Bristol, Scottish?
CHERYL	No no. European.
MATTHEW	Polish? Czech?
CHERYL	I don't know the difference between those ones.

MATTHEW   Was he good?

CHERYL   Oh very good.

            So this is where she wants to start.

MATTHEW   Yep. Now it's cleared. She wants to get
            planting.

CHERYL   What's she like then?

MATTHEW   You've met her.

CHERYL   You've spent more time. She's about the garden
            rather than the house.

MATTHEW   She's formidable. Attractive. For her age. Bone
            structure. Good figure.

CHERYL   Yes alright, I have *seen* her Matthew I'm
            talking about her personality.

MATTHEW   She grew up here. Well. Not grew up, but her
            uncle lived here when she was young and she
            remembers visiting.

CHERYL   Her uncle? That's why she's bought it then.

            Beat.

            It's a big job. This garden. Been left to ruin
            under your watch.

MATTHEW   Not my fault.

CHERYL   Not what it was.

MATTHEW   It needs resources.

CHERYL   Proper shithole these days.

            Beat.

            At least it went to someone who'll appreciate it.

            A moment.

MATTHEW   You feeling alright then?

CHERYL   Mind your own business.

MATTHEW   Good.

              A moment.

CHERYL   Who's her uncle then?

MATTHEW   Stanley Upthorne.

CHERYL   Stanley Upthorne. Well! So she's his niece.

              Funny how things come full circle isn't it?

              MATTHEW *rolls his eyes.*

              What?

MATTHEW   Fatuous thing to say.

CHERYL   Well it is.

MATTHEW   Meaningless.

CHERYL   Shut your face.

              ZARA *enters. She's twenty-two. Well turned
              out. Not used to the countryside.*

ZARA   Oh. Hello.

CHERYL   Matthew this is Zara, Mrs Walters' daughter.
              This is my husband Matthew. He does the
              garden here.

ZARA   Really?

MATTHEW   Twenty years now, on and off.

ZARA   Just you?

MATTHEW   That's right, and I know what you're thinking
              but the former owner didn't want so many hours
              putting in, is the truth. Couldn't afford it. But
              your mother, well she's pretty much asked for
              me full time. So it's all change. Big plans. You're
              living here too then? Come from London.

ZARA   Muswell Hill.

MATTHEW   Oh right. Didn't want to stay there?

ZARA   Yeah. I mean all my friends. Work. Opportunity,
              are there. Had the next few years all planned out
              then suddenly Mum sold the house and said
              we're moving to the country. I mean I get it's
              something that's important to her, but for me it's
              a disaster. Middle of nowhere.

CHERYL   Town's only two miles away.

ZARA   Two miles.

CHERYL   Not long in the car.

ZARA   I can't drive.

MATTHEW   Neither can she. Not properly. She put the
              wrong petrol in yesterday.

CHERYL   Oh be quiet.

ZARA   Can you walk it?

MATTHEW   Two miles? Of course. If you've got the time.

              ZARA *looks into the distance.*

ZARA   I like the flowers. There's nothing going on at the
              moment is there? In the garden, except weeds
              and grass but by the house there's a clump of.
              Like. White flowers.

MATTHEW   Snowdrops.

ZARA   Right.

MATTHEW   Early this year. Used to be swathes apparently.
              Your mum says they were everywhere,
              although I think that's unlikely. Either way, she
              wants them back.

              That'll cost her mind, if she can't wait for us to
              split them.

ZARA   She's obsessed.

MATTHEW   Nothing wrong with a hobby.

ZARA   It's more than that. Never seen her like it.

A moment.

MATTHEW   Well. I should get a move on. So should you
             woman, guests today. Sure you've got things to
             do. See you soon miss.

ZARA   Bye.

             They go. ZARA's left alone for a second.
             She looks around, sits and takes out a packet
             of cigarettes. She's about to smoke when
             GABRIEL *appears.*

GABRIEL   Oh.

ZARA   You alright?

GABRIEL   I'm Gabriel. From the house. Over there. The
             lady, the new owner. I used to do the windows
             here. I said I'm happy to keep… She said to
             come round to talk about it?

ZARA   I'm her daughter, Zara.

GABRIEL   Gabriel.

ZARA   You said.

             A moment.

GABRIEL   I live just over there. The house – you can see
             it, just about. See the roof? Live with my mum.
             I clean windows for some extra money. Not
             what I want to do. Eventually. But. You know.

ZARA   Yeah.

GABRIEL   You grew up in London.

             Beat.

             I always think you can tell if someone grew up
             in London. I mean we're not that far away here.
             Hour on the train or whatever, but it's so
             different. Someone grows up in London it's like
             they've got an extra layer. Of skin. Harder
             somehow.

ZARA	Harder.
GABRIEL	Like they've had to be that much tougher. Out here it's easy.
ZARA	I don't find it easy. How do you get anywhere? I don't drive.
GABRIEL	If you're going to live here you better learn. Taught my mate Chivers. He passed first time.

Beat.

What do you do then?

ZARA	I work in publishing.
GABRIEL	Cool. What as?
ZARA	Just done a placement in marketing, you know, it's not exactly what I want but... Been offered another in the children's section in the summer but not sure how I can afford that now – nowhere to live. I hope, she's going to help me out. Mum. Pay for somewhere in London. She ought to.
GABRIEL	I write. Like... short stories.
ZARA	Okay.
GABRIEL	So you're here for a while?

The doors open, and there's noise as AUDREY, PAUL *and* EDWARD, *all approach the garden.* ZARA *puts her cigarettes away quickly, and puts her sunglasses on.*

ZARA	Don't tell them I smoke.
GABRIEL	Okay.
AUDREY	...and down there was the long walk, which you can see in the photographs was framed with a magnificent structure they called Heaven's Gate. I just about remember it – the metal's frozen up now, but I remember the touch of

them, along with my grandfather's pipe smoke, crumpets on the terrace, the lily pond. It's overgrown, but still there, which is a huge bonus. It's going to take a while to sort out those gates, cost a fortune but it all must be done. Hello dear. Who's this?

ZARA   Gabriel.

GABRIEL   You… asked about window cleaning? I used to do it for the previous owners.

AUDREY   Oh. Yes… Did we arrange…

GABRIEL   I was passing.

AUDREY   Impromptu. Charming. What did you charge the previous?

GABRIEL   Thirty pounds.

AUDREY   How often?

GABRIEL   Once a month.

AUDREY   I'd like it done every week. And I'll pay forty, if you do it properly. The windows were a state when I arrived. I'm not just talking sloshing the water on, I mean get in there. Sparkling. Do you do Edward's? They look alright.

EDWARD   I do my own.

AUDREY   Oh.

EDWARD   Always have but Gabriel's a hard worker. I assume he hadn't cleaned them for a while as Mrs Gosford the previous owner, she was in hospital.

GABRIEL   That's right she said no point touching them while she was away.

EDWARD   He'll work hard.

PAUL   He'll take the forty pounds though, I'm sure.

GABRIEL   Well…

PAUL	That's a yes.
AUDREY	Alright then. Probation. Give them a clean and we'll see.
GABRIEL	Thank you.
AUDREY	Good. Now are we having tea? Gabriel, excuse us –
ZARA	Gabriel we're having tea, would you like to stop for tea?
AUDREY	Zara –
GABRIEL	Oh. Well…
	Yes please.
PAUL	It's a little chilly.
AUDREY	Oh Paul.
PAUL	What?
AUDREY	Man up.
PAUL	'Man up'. Right. I could fetch a pullover?
AUDREY	I thought tea outside might be fun. Tea in the Red Garden, although you'd have no idea why it was called that would you? Go on, both of you guess. Do you know?
PAUL	I assume red flowers.
AUDREY	There are red flowers but that's not why.
EDWARD	How the light falls.
AUDREY	Guess again.
ZARA	Oh for Christ's sake just tell us.
AUDREY	Maybe I'll tell you later. Keep you interested! (Your voice is very unattractive when you snap like that, Zara.) The point is each room had a theme. An exploration. No English garden had investigated things like that. It was either

landscape or cottage. Albion was the first to fuse those two approaches. The chaos of nature in a formal setting. It's of vital historical importance, and… look at it! The quintessential English Country Garden, this was the first. Laurence Weatherbury's masterpiece. It's referred to in all the guides at the time as being absolutely radical and absolutely beautiful. And well… look at it now. You'd never know.

PAUL   My wife is on a mission.

EDWARD   Good! It's important to have purpose.

PAUL   That's what they say. But I've never found it to be the case. My life has had no purpose and I've been unbelievably happy. To have a goal simply leaves one open to failure and disappointment. To drift means one can only ever be constantly surprised.

AUDREY   It's because you're Spanish.

PAUL   I'm not *Spanish*.

AUDREY   Spanish blood on his mother's side.

PAUL   I'm as English as you.

AUDREY   Catholic. Fate. Not English Protestant morality based on hard work. That's the key distinction, Paul. You can be happy without purpose. But for the true English man or woman, that's tantamount to a sin.

PAUL   Piffle.

ZARA   Is Katherine here yet?

AUDREY   I can't believe you've never met her.

ZARA   Well I know a lot about her.

AUDREY   From me I suppose. She's been abroad a lot recently. She's a novelist.

ZARA   Mum!

AUDREY   What? What's the matter?

ZARA   I *told* you! I *know* who is she. I read her work at uni.

AUDREY   Did you?

ZARA   Everyone knows who she is. She's famous.

AUDREY   Is she? *No*. She never said.

ZARA   Well you wouldn't would you.

AUDREY   I would if I were famous. I'd make it clear otherwise my friends could look foolish.

GABRIEL   Katherine who?

ZARA   Katherine Sanchez.

GABRIEL   Katherine Sanchez?!

AUDREY   Oh don't tell me you've heard of her too!

ZARA   Mum! Everyone's heard of her.

AUDREY   Yes but he cleans the windows.

GABRIEL   I write as well.

AUDREY   He writes as well. Of course he does. What a cultured corner of the country this is.

            ANNA *enters with tea on a tray.*

            Anna! Alright?

ANNA   Yes fine thank you. Sorry that took a while, I couldn't find the milk.

AUDREY   But you discovered it eventually, well done.

ANNA   It was in the other fridge.

AUDREY   Yes.

ANNA   You have two fridges.

AUDREY   Yes. That alright with you?

ANNA   Whatever you need.

AUDREY   Quite. Thank you anyway for getting the tea.
          Down here please. Wonderful.

          She gestures to a small table, by a bench.
          ANNA *puts it down and goes to pour.*

          Let me be mother. Seeing as I am.

ANNA   Which one's this?

AUDREY   The Red Garden. I was just saying –

ANNA   And how many are there?

AUDREY   At last! Someone's interested. Originally
          thirty-one separate rooms, or compartments as
          Weatherbury called them. This garden can
          never be appreciated in one view. It had to be
          experienced as a journey –

ANNA   Who's Weatherby?

AUDREY   *Weatherbury.* The visionary, remarkable man
          who created this garden, from nothing, in the
          hot summer of 1923.

PAUL   She's been reading a book.

AUDREY   *Books,* plural actually Paul. And papers, letters.
          Even as a child I knew there was something
          about this place. And then when I heard it had
          been left to wrack and ruin…

ANNA   So what are you going to do with it?

AUDREY   Restore it.

ANNA   All of it?

AUDREY   In time.

ANNA   Why?

AUDREY   What?

          Well.

          It's important.

ANNA   To who?

AUDREY   Everyone. All of us.

            As AUDREY *continues,* ANNA *walks off
            a little away from the others, thinking.*

            We'll start here, with the Red Garden, and work
            out. The Red and the Pool Garden are this
            year's projects.

PAUL   Do you remember it Edward?

EDWARD   I remember it being talked about but I never
            visited when the garden was still being
            preserved well. I mean that was the irony
            actually, Mrs Walters your uncle kept the place
            meticulously, having bought it directly from
            Weatherbury himself in his later years, and
            keeping it thus he insisted on privacy. He felt
            too many visitors would trammel and trample
            the work. When he sold it on, the new owner,
            Cartwright didn't have the same means, so he
            turfed a lot of it, but it meant the village fête
            could be held here, parties, weddings. There's
            quite an expectation Mrs Walters as you're no
            doubt aware. This garden has developed into an
            important amenity for the village.

AUDREY   Yes I've heard about that.

EDWARD   There's one event every summer where people
            volunteer and dress up as characters from
            books, and the local children have to find them
            in the nooks and crannies of the garden, it's
            beautiful.

GABRIEL   I did that, last year.

ZARA   Who were you?

GABRIEL   Cat in the Hat.

            A moment.

AUDREY   Well it may not be compatible with my plans.
            There's delicate work to do here, and certainly
            while we're doing that work, the village may
            have to find another venue.

EDWARD   Surely just a few days a year.

AUDREY   My garden, Edward.

PAUL   Our garden.

AUDREY   Our garden, my husband and me, and we have
            to feel we own it.

EDWARD   I'm sure no one will intrude.

AUDREY   It's not about lack of generosity and community,
            we'll play our part in some other way, I'm sure,
            but this is a larger project now, something of
            national importance, to restore this vital part of
            our heritage. Now. Who's for tea? Zara?

            She pours.

ZARA   Have you got sugar?

AUDREY   Of course.

ZARA   You cut it out for ages.

AUDREY   Yes we're over that now.

ZARA   Two please.

AUDREY   How are you not obese? It's certainly not
            exercise, lounging around. I should put you to
            work. Do half a day's digging, make a woman
            out of you. Some germs in your system. Some
            earth. Lived in the city all your life, never got
            your hands dirty.

ZARA   And you have?

AUDREY   I grew up in the country.

ZARA   Reading.

AUDREY   Outskirts.

ZARA   Mum you've been in a boardroom your entire
            adult life.

AUDREY   But all that time, I knew what a garden was.
            Might have just been that patch of concrete
            and pots on our terrace but I've been gardening
            all my life, in one way or – What's the matter
            with you?

ZARA   A little bored I suppose.

AUDREY   Bored! It's like having a fifteen-year-old again!
            You need things to happen all the time don't
            you? All these screens, no concentration. I've
            told you, invite a friend or something. Meet a
            boy. I don't know. You do have friends I assume?

ZARA   Not out here.

AUDREY   Well make some! Lots of young people in the
            village.

            ZARA *rolls her eyes*.

ZARA   'Young people'.

            AUDREY *hands the tea out*.

AUDREY   And there's Anna. She's not young I know, but
            she's here.

PAUL   This is a terrible risk for us. Had to give up our
            London house to afford it. And you know what
            they say.

            'Once you leave London, you'll never get
            back in.'

ZARA   I'm going back.

PAUL   Once you get off the London ladder, so this was
            a big mistake in that sense, everyone said it,
            especially as things are, but as with so many
            things, there was no persuading her. Not that
            I tried particularly.

            Like trying to stop the weather.

> ANNA *stands and goes up to* AUDREY.

ANNA   Where's James?

AUDREY   I'm sorry?

ANNA   He wasn't on the side, where he was in your old house, in the, what do you call it... living room.

AUDREY   Drawing room.

PAUL   This is all new, by the way, drawing room rather than living room, terrace rather than patio.

AUDREY   This is how I was brought up, before I was corrupted by my first husband, my son, my daughter and now by you Anna, we've still got a lot boxed up in that room, particularly the most valuable items, as we're moving things round and we didn't want anything broken.

ANNA   Can you find him?

AUDREY   Yes, of course.

ANNA   Before I go.

AUDREY   Yes, we'll... find him later.

ZARA   When's Katherine getting here?

AUDREY   Any minute I think, but it's alright, Cheryl can open the door, we don't stand on ceremony, wait around for her, she'll make herself at home, always has before.

EDWARD   How are you finding Cheryl?

PAUL   Who's Cheryl?

AUDREY   Oh Paul!

PAUL   What?

AUDREY   The *cleaner.*

PAUL   Right yes, *Cheryl! S*o many new people. Well she's nice. Don't you think?

AUDREY   She's fine.

EDWARD   She does how many days?

AUDREY   Three days a week.

EDWARD   Right. Right.

            A moment.

AUDREY   Why do you ask?

EDWARD   Only because she used to do mine, and said she
            needed two days, but then we got recommended
            this new girl, Krystyna. She came in, did a
            better job in half the time. Whirling dervish,
            runs round, does it all. The problem with
            Cheryl is she's rather... well... slow.

AUDREY   She's worked here a long time.

EDWARD   Oh well that's true. And with Matthew as well...
            but I thought I'd mention it, as Krystyna's round
            at mine at the moment, I could send her across.

PAUL   'Cheryl' always wants cash. Last couple of
            weeks I've asked if I can transfer the money,
            and she was adamant it had to be notes, so she
            cleans me out, if I have it, or I have to drive to
            get it. Not a huge thing, but you know...

EDWARD   Krystyna's all above board. Her own business.
            She employs other people. Very enterprising.

            Beat.

AUDREY   Ask her to come over and see us once she's
            finished at yours. But obviously tell her not to
            say why she's here.

EDWARD   Of course.

AUDREY   Right then, who would like to hear the grand
            plan. Edward? Yes?

EDWARD   Oh absolutely.

AUDREY   Paul you've heard it before but it won't do any
            harm to have a repeat.

PAUL   I'll just think about other things.

AUDREY   Zara? Come on, I know you're interested.

ZARA   I'm staying here.

AUDREY   Gabriel?

GABRIEL   Oh. I don't –

AUDREY   Zara will show you out. I look forward to the
                windows.

GABRIEL   I'll… I came in through the gate at the bottom
                so –

AUDREY   Oh.

GABRIEL   My house is down the Croft. Is it alright if I go
                out that way?

AUDREY   You let yourself in?

GABRIEL   I used to with the previous. But whatever you'd
                like.

ZARA   Oh Mum come on let him use the gate, it's
                a long way round otherwise.

AUDREY   Well alright but… let me know when you're
                coming, for the windows.

GABRIEL   Absolutely.

AUDREY   Just so it doesn't become a thoroughfare. Anna?

ANNA   No thanks.

AUDREY   Just the ancients then! This way… perhaps
                we'll find Matthew as we go…

                She leads EDWARD *and* PAUL *off.* ANNA *sits
                on the other bench.* ZARA *enjoys the sun.*
                GABRIEL *finishes his tea.*

GABRIEL   What did you mean? James. You said you
                couldn't find James. What's James?

                A moment.

ZARA   James died two years ago.

ANNA   My partner. Her brother.

GABRIEL   Oh. I'm sorry. How?

ZARA   He was a captain. In the army. Killed by
            a roadside bomb.

GABRIEL   God. So you were talking about…

ZARA   His ashes. He didn't leave instructions with
            what to do with them. Mum's keeping them
            while we all make a plan.

GABRIEL   For two years?

            They look at him. Exactly.

            It becomes an awkward moment.

            I should leave.

ZARA   Good to meet you.

GABRIEL   You too. Will you… excuse me. But Katherine
            Sanchez, she's one of my favourite writers. If
            I brought back a book, do you think you could
            ask her to sign it?

ZARA   Yeah of course. Drop it round.

GABRIEL   I'll go home and get it now.

            Thanks.

            He hurries off. A moment. Then ZARA *gets out
            her cigarettes.*

            Beat.

ZARA   Impressive. Visiting us all the way out here.

ANNA   He only gave me a few bits and pieces when we
            were together. But most of his possessions, his
            childhood things, you know textbooks from
            school, his teenage stuff, she saved it all,
            hoarded it, it's all here, and she's keeping hold
            of it, so the only way I get to spend time with
            him is being in her house.

ZARA   Even though you can't stand her.

ANNA   James said there was something underneath.
            To give her a chance. That one day I'd see
            through the façade and realise what she really
            was, and that I'd like that.

ZARA   You could be waiting a long time.

            I liked your idea of the journey of his life. A little
            bit in every place that meant something to him.

ANNA   She won't have it. Says that would split him up.

ZARA   He's already split up though isn't he?
            Thousands of pieces. Let's keep trying.

ANNA   Yes. Thanks. Thank you.

            A moment.

ZARA   It's a different world out here. Even the birds
            seem to move faster in London. I thought it
            might be like being on holiday all the time. I'd
            settle and start writing, like I'd always intended.
            But no. With more time to think, I think less.

ANNA   I don't mind it so far actually. Welcome break
            from work. I like the view.

            A moment.

ZARA   Met anyone?

ANNA   No.

ZARA   You were going to try a dating thing. App.

ANNA   I'd have to learn how they work.

ZARA   I know. I've reverted to the standard. Parties,
            drunk, back to mine. But either way, it's dull
            really. Truth is I don't know what I'm after.

            ANNA *looks at her and smiles.*

ANNA   You're so young.

ZARA   You too.

ANNA   No.

                KATHERINE SANCHEZ *comes out of the*
                house.

KATHERINE   Hello! I was told you're all out here! I'm
                Katherine, I assume one of you must be Zara.
                I'm going to say... you.

ZARA   Yes. Really pleased to meet you.

KATHERINE   Wonderful to meet *you*! A little like your
                mother when she was young only prettier,
                thinner. Should I say slimmer? Not saying that's
                a bad thing, it's clearly the fashion. Attractive
                anyway. Hello.

ZARA   This is Anna. James's partner.

KATHERINE   Ah yes. Of course. Awful. I'm so sorry.

ANNA   Thank you.

KATHERINE   You both responded to the invitation did you?

ANNA   I did. Zara moved with her mum.

KATHERINE   Not staying in London? Surely you'd rather be
                there at your age.

ZARA   I thought I might like it here instead.

KATHERINE   But you don't.

ZARA   ...

KATHERINE   So this is it! The famous garden. I've seen
                better. Just come back from South Africa, and
                I found myself just walking through the hills,
                searching for something, god knows if I found
                it. But you have to keep looking, don't you?
                Only way you'll progress.

ANNA   Do you want a drink?

KATHERINE   Yes please, if you're offering, gin and tonic.
                Is that on the cards? This looks like tea, but I'd
                prefer a spiky one if it's possible.

ANNA	Absolutely.
KATHERINE	Thank you.

ANNA *goes inside*.

Yes, South Africa – can't remember what I was saying. What was I saying?

ZARA You have to keep looking.

A moment. KATHERINE *looks at* ZARA, *impressed*.

KATHERINE Well remembered.

ZARA Can I confess something?

KATHERINE So soon?

ZARA I'm a big fan. You're the reason I'm still here. A friend offered me to live with them for a few weeks, but Mum said you were visiting, and we always miss each other and I thought this time no. I want to meet you.

KATHERINE Really?

ZARA I… I've just done a placement in publishing I just… adore books, words, you know, ever since I was young. And your work in particular, it speaks to me. What your characters, these central characters go through, as women, there's no better articulation of the female experience.

KATHERINE You think so?

ZARA I… I wrote a number of essays, at university, on your early novels.

KATHERINE Darling! Where did you go?

ZARA Trinity. Cambridge.

KATHERINE You know I've never really intended my protagonists to be women. It just happens like that.

ZARA   Really?

KATHERINE   I write the person, and they're a woman, but
                they could equally one day be a man, I'm sure.
                It's the story that drives me. The narrative.

                Beat.

ZARA   Your life must be... incredible!

KATHERINE   Well...

ZARA   Sorry. But I'm so jealous. You don't take
                commissions, advances, do you?

KATHERINE   That's right.

ZARA   So you can stay completely independent. You
                just live and write and when you're ready you
                release the book and it makes enough for you to
                live and travel and do it all over again. And
                that's always been the case for you.

KATHERINE   – yes since I was twenty-five, twenty-six maybe.

ZARA   You must have such adventures. In interviews
                you talk about what you've done. Your life, and
                how that feeds in.

                I'd like to write.

                KATHERINE *looks at* ZARA.

KATHERINE   Adventures...? Hmm.

                I must be honest with you Zara. I pretend. After
                I've written I make up stories to justify my
                choices, because people do like to hear that
                fiction comes from personal experience, but I'm
                actually very shy. My life has been lived
                watching other people living, really, always
                feeling I'm on the outskirts of life, never at the
                heart. I was never pretty enough to land the
                boy, or the girl. Always left the party too early,
                or was in the wrong room, missed the big event.
                I think that's what drives my work, not a life of
                adventure but a life of imagining what I missed.

You won't understand. You're far too pretty.
Life will come to you. I'm sure it already has.
Life will give you opportunity, especially
because of your mother, but you're clever and
very attractive. The truth is you'll struggle to be
a writer.

ZARA   I know! I don't think I ever could be! Not after
I read your work, I thought – just give up –

KATHERINE   I'm flattered but that's not the reason. You'll
never be a writer because you don't need to be.
You are accepted, loved, unlike me, your life
will be by default, full. Just look at you.

ZARA   I don't know. I'll get well-paid work, an editor,
an agent something like that, I'm sure I could.
But I'm worried. I went from St Mary's to
Trinity, to work placements, with skiing and
beaches in between, and I'm starting to think –
oh god this is a champagne problem I know, as
I've been sat here in this garden, that maybe
I'm in a bubble. Maybe I haven't met real
people. Maybe I've been closed off from the
world my entire life.

I'm after a dream. A sense of purpose, I suppose.

KATHERINE   Then what do you believe in? You can't have
purpose without belief.

ZARA *looks at her, then puts out her cigarette.*

Does your mother know you smoke?

ZARA   Shit – No. Please don't tell her. I don't know
why I do it. All my friends are stopping. Or
never started. It's a dirty habit.

KATHERINE   Maybe that's what you're craving:

A little imperfection.

Beat.

AUDREY   You're actually here!

AUDREY *and* PAUL *have come back.*
AUDREY *greets* KATHERINE. ZARA *puts the packet away.*

KATHERINE   I am! How are you?!

AUDREY   I'm thriving! Blooming! So's Paul.

PAUL   Nonsense. I'm exactly the same but outdoors. Hello!

AUDREY   He's got more vitamin D in the last two weeks than his whole life, out walking the whole time.

PAUL   Nothing else to do.

AUDREY   Well that's not true. He's joined a curry club. The men in the village they go out for curry. For Paul that's huge. You were never the social butterfly in London.

PAUL   Well. I like curry.

KATHERINE   I think it's marvellous! What a decision!

AUDREY   A deficient house and a pretty rough patch of earth. However it's a start – and that's something you taught me Katherine. Follow your dreams. A wonderful motto.

KATHERINE   Taught by rote, I fear, rather than example. I was just saying, my dreams are fantasies. My life a shadow.

AUDREY   You two have spoken then. Yes. Thought you might get on, this tendency to melancholy. She tells me you're famous.

KATHERINE   Amongst a certain kind of Cambridge graduate, maybe.

AUDREY   No there was a boy here, he also knew who you were, I had no idea. You speak at events, go on Radio 4, that kind of thing?

KATHERINE   Sometimes.

AUDREY   How come I've never heard of you?

KATHERINE   Well... you've been busy I'm sure.

We live in different worlds Aud.

ZARA   Where's the neighbour?

AUDREY   Gone home. Thought we'd just want family now.

KATHERINE   Then I should go.

AUDREY   Oh Katherine you *are* family. Do you have a drink?

KATHERINE   I ordered a G and T.

ZARA   Anna went. Are we definitely staying out here?

AUDREY   Yes! It's better than the house. Paul get some chairs out darling, and tell Anna to make it gin and tonics all round.

PAUL   Right... Right.

He goes.

AUDREY   We're celebrating!

ZARA   Celebrating what?

KATHERINE *looks to* ZARA.

KATHERINE   Dreams.

AUDREY   Precisely.

Weatherbury said this was a house to dream of, and a garden to dream in.

CHERYL *enters.*

CHERYL   Excuse me. There's a lady at the door called Krystyna. Apparently you have a mutual friend and you said to stop by.

AUDREY   Oh, yes, I'll... actually, can you send her out here.

CHERYL   Right...

AUDREY   Thank you!

            She goes.

            Gosh. Awks! She's a possible new cleaner. Now
            I've got to interview the replacement under the
            nose of the current.

KATHERINE   Oh, Aud you really are living out your fantasy
            aren't you? A landowner with difficult staff.
            You'll be getting the croquet out next.

ZARA   She's bought a set!

KATHERINE   No!

AUDREY   What's wrong with that?

KATHERINE   Nothing! I think it's delightful. Never seen you
            like this. You're right. You are blooming. You
            would've been happy with staff.

AUDREY   My uncle had staff when he was here. I
            remember being fascinated when we came to
            visit. Where did they go?! But no, I mean all
            that... long gone... although I do find myself
            thinking what exactly is wrong with it? As long
            as they're paid well, are happy in their jobs,
            they would have more security than a courier or
            one of those Uber drivers. A part of me doesn't
            understand why it's politically incorrect.

ZARA   Not incorrect any more, it's making a comeback.

KATHERINE   I bet a lot of your friends had servants,
            growing up.

ZARA   Yeah. Cleaners. Nannies. Housekeepers.

KATHERINE   I suppose the objection is it's in your home.
            It's helping you with things that most people
            have no trouble doing themselves.

AUDREY   Well that's simply not true – people have
            enormous trouble keeping their house clean,
            looking after their children while working.

KATHERINE   You can justify almost anything with practicality.

KRYSTYNA comes in.

KRYSTYNA   Hi.

AUDREY   Krystyna?

KRYSTYNA   Hello.

AUDREY   Audrey Walters. This is my daughter Zara, my friend Katherine, thank you for being discreet, you'll understand why of course. I thought Cheryl would have left before you came over but…

KRYSTYNA   You don't want to upset her.

AUDREY   How astute of you.

KATHERINE   Where are you from Krystyna?

KRYSTYNA   Poland originally. I've been here three years now. I am with my boyfriend.

KATHERINE   And what does he do?

KRYSTYNA   He is getting ready. We're starting a business together.

KATHERINE   Really? Here?

KRYSTYNA smiles.

KRYSTYNA   No.

A shadow passes. PAUL enters with two extra chairs.

PAUL   Gin and tonic on its way. Hello.

AUDREY   This is Krystyna –

KRYSTYNA   Hello.

PAUL   I'm the husband. You know Cheryl's still –

AUDREY   Yes yes, it's fine.

(*To* KRYSTYNA.) A house of this size, how long would you think it would take?

KRYSTYNA   How many bedrooms?

AUDREY   Seven bedrooms. Three bathrooms.

PAUL   Four.

AUDREY   Really?

PAUL   Oh yes. Four bathrooms. Tried them all. As
             I said, there really is nothing to do.

             PAUL *leaves again.*

KRYSTYNA   Maybe a full day, I would say to clean it all.

AUDREY   Just a day.

KRYSTYNA   I would get my friend in to help, the two of us
             would do it in five hours, so we would charge
             you ten hours at twelve pounds an hour.
             Something like that.

AUDREY   Do you have availability?

KRYSTYNA   Yes, I could do a Thursday at the moment.

AUDREY   Alright. Can I get your number?

KRYSTYNA   I have a card.

KATHERINE   A card?! How organised.

KRYSTYNA   It's my business.

KATHERINE   Of course.

KRYSTYNA   I know who you are by the way.

AUDREY   You... you do?

KRYSTYNA   Yes my boyfriend, he got me a present from one
             of your shops. A tablecloth?

AUDREY   Oh good.

KRYSTYNA   We like it. It's white.

KATHERINE   Of course! It's all white. Everything's white in
             her shop. That's her thing.

AUDREY   Katherine –

KATHERINE   Even the customers.

AUDREY   Oh please! Your boyfriend has good taste.

KRYSTYNA   Yes we like it a lot. And I like that you made
                the business yourself.

AUDREY   Do you? Good.

KRYSTYNA   I'll wait to hear from you.

AUDREY   It won't be long.

KRYSTYNA   Thank you.

                She goes.

AUDREY   Clever young woman.

                (*To* KATHERINE.) Cheryl's been here twenty
                years is the problem, and her husband knows
                the garden well. Can't afford to lose him.

KATHERINE   Oh the troubles you have.

AUDREY   I know, I know but this is my life and the truth
                is, believe it or not, both of you, for I see the
                scepticism in your collective face, the truth is
                I don't actually like to upset people.

KATHERINE   You may have to adjust your plans for the
                climate.

AUDREY   You mean now we've –

KATHERINE   I mean the planting. When Weatherbury chose
                his plants it was a hundred years ago. The
                climate will be quite different now. Sun like this
                in early February. Unheard of back then. We're
                becoming the South of France.

AUDREY   Oh I hope so. Means we won't have to actually
                go there any more. No offence, and I know the
                cheese and landscape and whatever, but the
                people. My god! So rude. And it's nothing to do
                with language. My French is excellent. But all
                that means is I can appreciate their rudeness
                with even more subtlety.

                Beat.

Weatherbury had a house in Menton on the Riviera, but it was his mother who used it. He stayed here. And I know precisely why. It may have been hotter there, and more serene, but this place has the romance, the moods, like ourselves. It's England really isn't it? A climate without cloud and rain isn't honest.

KATHERINE   You love it here.

AUDREY   I do. As a child there were a number of big houses in the area. When we'd visit the adults would dress up in the evenings – us children would listen at the top of the stairs. It was the seventies but it felt timeless – the music playing, the clatter of cutlery, and then after they would retreat to their private conversations, in halls, in drawing rooms, or out on summer nights, down through the private rooms of the garden to the bathing pond, or the infinity walk. And I thought when I grew up that would be the world I'd inherit, but then it was the eighties, and it was all... destroyed. It's easy to mock but there was a culture there. Most other countries preserve their past. The embarrassed and insecure English discard it. And then complain when the replacement isn't any good.

A moment. KATHERINE *watching* AUDREY.

What?

KATHERINE   How are you?

AUDREY   I'm fine.

Beat.

KATHERINE   I'm so sorry.

AUDREY   Thank you.

KATHERINE   I don't know how you coped. All of you.

AUDREY   Well, when something like that happens, you
                just carry on, don't you? You rely on each other.
                Family. Friends.

                Beat.

                Of course we always knew it was possible.
                And his passing on, at least it meant something.
                He died for a purpose, in service to his country.
                I hold onto that, and it keeps me steady.

KATHERINE   And Anna's his –

AUDREY   His partner, at the time.

KATHERINE   And she's visiting?

AUDREY   She sees us quite a bit.

ZARA   She's nice.

AUDREY   She's a little… what's the word?

                Vulnerable?

                PAUL *enters, helped by* CHERYL, *with a jug
                of gin and tonic, and two extra chairs. They lay
                them out.*

PAUL   Here we are. Thank you Cheryl.

AUDREY   You've mixed it already?

PAUL   I have. As usual.

AUDREY   What if people wanted different strengths?

PAUL   Is everyone happy to trust me on strength?

KATHERINE   Yes.

ZARA   Absolutely.

PAUL   Turns out we're fine. Thank you Cheryl, that's
                perfect!

                PAUL *does a look to* AUDREY – *this is
                horrible.*

CHERYL   Alright, well I'm done for the day, so I'll see
              you tomorrow. You're alright to pay tomorrow?
              Cash if possible.

PAUL   I'll get it first thing.

CHERYL   Appreciate it.

              She goes. PAUL *makes sure she's out the way,*
              then turns to the others.

PAUL   Well we're in a bit of spot I'd say. She went for
              a scan last Friday, after they found a lump.
              She's got an appointment on Thursday to
              discuss it.

AUDREY   Cancer?

PAUL   Maybe.

AUDREY   Jesus.

PAUL   I know.

AUDREY   Why did you tell me?! I could have called her
              tonight, let her go, and pretend I don't know.
              I can't fire her the week she's got cancer!

PAUL   She *might* have cancer.

KATHERINE   Why do you need to fire her anyway?

AUDREY   Because I'm paying someone to potter aimless
              round my house for three days not-particularly-
              cleaning when it could all be done in one, it
              offends my business instinct.

KATHERINE   Aud! She's got cancer!

ZARA   Probably.

PAUL   Possibly.

AUDREY   This has got ridiculous.

PAUL   Try not to worry about it. Here.

AUDREY   Where's Anna?

PAUL	I don't know.
AUDREY	Can't get everyone in the same place! It's a special day and I wanted to say a few words.
PAUL	Shall I go and get her?
AUDREY	No she'll work it out, I'm sure.
	GABRIEL *enters*.
GABRIEL	Oh.
AUDREY	Gabriel? You're not doing the windows now.
GABRIEL	No. I... sorry –
ZARA	He wanted to get his book signed by Katherine. I told him to go and get it, bring it back.
AUDREY	Well she's here for a week. Can't he...
ZARA	Oh Mum it's fine Gabriel come on. Come and meet her. Do you want a gin and tonic?
AUDREY	Zara –
GABRIEL	Well. Only if it's...
ZARA	Course you do. This is Katherine.
KATHERINE	Hello.
GABRIEL	I'm, a huge fan.
AUDREY	Oh for crying out loud –
KATHERINE	Thank you Gabriel. What a lovely name.
AUDREY	Do you get this a lot?
GABRIEL	Would it be alright to...
KATHERINE	Of course.
AUDREY	How do you cope with it?
KATHERINE	It's a privilege Audrey, that people read your work and like it. I assume it's the same when you meet people who like shopping in your shop.

AUDREY   Well not particularly, they don't revere me –

KATHERINE   Not true. That girl. Krystyna. She knew who
            you were. She was impressed.

AUDREY   Yes but you didn't see her blushing, not like
            this. Look at him! A tomato.

ZARA   Stop being mean!

AUDREY   Why? Have you got an interest you'd like to
            declare?

ZARA   Ignore her.

            She gives him a gin and tonic.

GABRIEL   Thank you.

KATHERINE   You like this one?

GABRIEL   Yes, my favourite.

KATHERINE   I've just finished a new one.

GABRIEL   Really?

KATHERINE   Yes.

GABRIEL   Will you tell me about it?

KATHERINE   Well... yes of course.

AUDREY   Maybe not now?

KATHERINE   Later. I promise.

GABRIEL   Thank you.

            KATHERINE *turns to* AUDREY.

KATHERINE   This is a big undertaking. Are you sure you're
            up to it yourself. What about your work?

AUDREY   I'm still part of it. Just stepped back from a few
            more time-consuming things.

GABRIEL   If you need any help?

AUDREY   Sorry?

GABRIEL   I've got this year. I want to go to uni and I need
             to earn money. If you wanted any help with the
             garden.

AUDREY   Well speak to Matthew.

GABRIEL   Alright.

             ANNA *enters*.

AUDREY   Anna, sweetheart. Here, have a gin and tonic.
             Now before anyone else disappears –

             She looks at GABRIEL.

             – or appears, I just wanted to say a few words,
             to start this project, on this day, the very day –

ANNA   I asked Cheryl about the drawing room, she
             said the urn was in there, on the side, that she
             would remember something like that, but today
             it's gone.

ZARA   Gone?

ANNA   Where is he? Why did you lie?

             A moment. Everyone looking at AUDREY.

AUDREY   Oh Anna! There's no conspiracy, alright, look
             I removed it up to my room, I just felt he was
             a bit exposed down there and with everyone /
             coming today and –

ANNA   I searched your room –

AUDREY   You searched…

ANNA   After you lied, I needed to know where he was,
             and I found the urn but his ashes aren't in there
             any more.

             Where is he?

AUDREY   I would appreciate it if you didn't speak to me
             like this.

ANNA   I'm asking a simple question –

AUDREY   Your voice is raised, your face is hot and
          I don't –

ANNA   You're hiding something.

AUDREY   You feel there's some great mystery?

ANNA   Where is he?

AUDREY   Anna.

ANNA   *Don't lie.*

ZARA   Mum?

          AUDREY *smiles.*

AUDREY   Alright. I hoped we wouldn't have to have this
          conversation so publicly but the truth is this
          to-ing and fro-ing about how we're going to
          scatter them has caused me a lot of stress, a lot
          of sleepless nights, I have to tell you.

          (*To* PAUL.) I haven't been sleeping, have I?

PAUL   What?

AUDREY   I've been awake in the night worrying.

PAUL   Oh well, yes, you have.

AUDREY   *Yes.* So to cut a long story short, yesterday
          evening, I was here in the garden, I'd had a
          couple of glasses of wine over dinner, and I was
          making plans, and I got quite sad. I read about
          the fact that this garden was a tribute from
          Weatherbury to his fallen colleagues and
          friends who never made it home from the First
          World War. Who made the ultimate sacrifice for
          England. Weatherbury was a captain in the
          army as well you know. The same as James.

ANNA   What have you done?

AUDREY   I'm telling you! Weatherbury was shot at Ypres,
          put on the pile of the dead, and it was only
          because a passing private happened to see his
          body move that he was pulled out, and brought

back to life. And that's why it's called the Red Garden, because it's about blood.

It's what he saw on the battlefield. This garden was a tribute to those soldiers who were devoted to their country but weren't so lucky to come back to it. And James is one of those soldiers –

ANNA   No.

AUDREY   – so I came and scattered him. Here. Last night.

A shocked silence.

As the plants grow, as this garden blooms every year, we can remember him.

ANNA   But I should have… He was going to be my husband.

AUDREY   With respect you don't know that, there was no formal –

ANNA   He's Zara's brother.

AUDREY   Zara doesn't mind.

ZARA   …

AUDREY   Do you?

ZARA   You should have spoken to us Mum.

AUDREY   Alright, well I didn't, and it's done. But at least either way our problem is resolved. I'm sorry you don't like my solution. But he's my son, ultimately. I gave birth to him. He had me from the beginning. He has me at the end.

A moment. ANNA *sits in one of the chairs, shocked. Drinks her drink.*

Then reaches down and touches the ground.

A moment. AUDREY *uncomfortable.*

Leading to…

You're welcome to visit whenever you want. To come here.

ANNA   Whenever I want?

                AUDREY *regrets it already.*

AUDREY   Of course.

                A moment.

                They drink. A cloud passes over.

                PAUL *looks up.*

PAUL   Look.

KATHERINE   Sorry?

PAUL   The sun. It's gone.

                End of Act One.

ACT TWO

Late May. A summer's evening.

The same garden, but now the plants have grown up, and one can see the outline. The beds, the paths. It's becoming beautiful.

Over the course of the act, the sun sets, and the final moments take place in mostly moonlight.

We hear the sound of a gramophone playing 1920s music, from the house.

GABRIEL, *in 1920s black tie, walks into the garden. He looks around, then takes out his small notebook from his inside pocket and writes.*

Behind him, KRYSTYNA *appears. She's dressed as a 1920s maid and is holding a tray of drinks.*

KRYSTYNA   Another?

GABRIEL   Thank you.

             He takes one. She makes to go.

             Will you?

KRYSTYNA   I'm working.

GABRIEL   I'm sure Mrs Walters wouldn't mind.

KRYSTYNA   Actually, she said I could have one if I liked.

GABRIEL   Right then.

             KRYSTYNA *smiles. Puts the tray down and takes a glass.*

             They drink.

             It's been such a success. She must be pleased with everything you've done.

KRYSTYNA   I hope so.

GABRIEL   Do you like it here?

KRYSTYNA   This area?

GABRIEL   Britain.

KRYSTYNA   Oh.

            It's okay.

GABRIEL   You feel welcome.

KRYSTYNA   Yes, I will never be British but there's been
            work for good money. That's all that matters.

GABRIEL   But with everything that's happened...?

            KRYSTYNA *smiles*.

KRYSTYNA   That's your problem.

            What are you writing?

GABRIEL   Oh. Nothing.

KRYSTYNA   Not nothing.

GABRIEL   Just notes for a story.

KRYSTYNA   A love story?

GABRIEL   What?

KRYSTYNA   You've been looking at Zara all night.

GABRIEL   No I haven't.

KRYSTYNA   You should try to make it less obvious.

            Beat.

GABRIEL   She looks older now, don't you think?

KRYSTYNA   She's your type.

GABRIEL   Well, she loves writing, and literature, and she's
            beautiful, so yes.

            But I don't know how to approach her. She's
            quite formidable.

KRYSTYNA   I don't understand. You should just speak to her.

GABRIEL   And say what?

KRYSTYNA   Tell her a story.

A moment.

GABRIEL   How old are you?

KRYSTYNA   Twenty-three.

GABRIEL   Twenty-three. Only four years older than me. And you've got your own business, contacts, you're making a lot of money. I've seen your car.

KRYSTYNA   I share it with my friend.

GABRIEL   Even so.

KRYSTYNA   I work hard. I make money, yes. Nothing wrong with that, is there?

ZARA comes out, with her cigarettes, and lights one. She's dressed as a 1920s flapper.

I should get back.

She goes. Leaving them alone. ZARA turns and sees GABRIEL.

ZARA   Gabriel!

GABRIEL   Hi. Hello.

She hugs him.

ZARA   (*Whilst hugging.*) Gabriel.

GABRIEL   That's right.

ZARA   You want?

GABRIEL   Oh. I… yes.

ZARA   You don't have to.

GABRIEL   No I… yes please.

ZARA   You've started?

GABRIEL   At parties.

*She gives him one, lights hers, then gives him the
lighter. After a couple of attempts he lights it.*

ZARA   Murderer!

GABRIEL   Yes.

ZARA   You did well.

GABRIEL   I was unbelievably nervous. I don't keep secrets
              very well. And, everyone was, there's some
              very powerful people in there.

ZARA   Powerful but boring. You should think more of
              yourself.

              Beat.

GABRIEL   You look amazing.

ZARA   Did my best to get in the spirit of it. This has
              grown.

GABRIEL   Yes takes a lot of work.

ZARA   You're a gardener now?

GABRIEL   Helping Matthew. He's had to take time out for
              his wife so... there's lots to do.

ZARA   How is she?

GABRIEL   Responding well apparently. Things are hard
              for them. Financially. No real pensions... All
              the travelling to appointments. We try to help
              when we can.

ZARA   We?

GABRIEL   Neighbours. In the village.

              How have you been?

ZARA   I did the placement. Been living with a friend in
              Herne Hill. She lets me camp in her spare room
              rent free. Says I can stay as long as I like.

GABRIEL   Met anyone?

ZARA   You mean…? Well. The odd… evening. But no.

              You're going to university?

GABRIEL   In September.

ZARA   Where?

GABRIEL   Probably Brookes. In Oxford. I can get the bus.

ZARA   Studying what?

GABRIEL   Creative writing. There's a good course, and
              agents come at the end, look over your stuff,
              I think it'll be good.

              Beat.

              What?

ZARA   You know I'm just not sure those courses are
              really worth very much. If you're going to get
              into all that debt, wouldn't you do better to take
              a degree which will be respected whatever you
              end up doing, for instance English Literature is
              a basis for all sorts of further education or
              careers, whatever, but creative writing is more or
              less useless if you don't go into actually being
              a writer, which, let's face it, most people don't.

GABRIEL   You think I should do English?

ZARA   You've got good A levels.

GABRIEL   A and two B's.

ZARA   Right. You could get in to do English
              somewhere easily.

GABRIEL   Brookes is really the only option.

ZARA   Oxford proper.

GABRIEL   I'd have to retake.

ZARA   Do that then.

GABRIEL   Too late for this year now. I don't want to have
              another year out.

ZARA   Fine then do English at Brookes.

GABRIEL	It's the agents. It's hard to get them to read anything.
ZARA	You just need to get it in front of them.
GABRIEL	Exactly.
ZARA	Well I could do that. I see them on my placements, meet them at events.
GABRIEL	Really?
ZARA	Course. Send me something.
GABRIEL	You... okay.

A moment.

I was writing a story just now actually.

ZARA	Really?
GABRIEL	About a woman with this amazing hair. She didn't appreciate the effect it had on people.
ZARA	Tell me.
GABRIEL	It put them in her power. She didn't realise that everyone around was in awe of her. And then when she got her hair cut, it all went away.
ZARA	How sad.
GABRIEL	It grows back so she's fine.
ZARA	No, that the only thing that interested people about her was her hair. Not her conversation, her intelligence.
GABRIEL	I think that's what I'm trying to get at. No one saw who she was underneath.
ZARA	And was she someone, underneath?
GABRIEL	...yes I think so.
ZARA	Some people aren't. Some people, you lift the lid, get behind the mask, and there's nothing there.

I think I might be like that.

GABRIEL   No.

ZARA   How would you know?

GABRIEL   I'm sure.

             You haven't got a drink.

             I'll get you one.

             I was wondering…

             KATHERINE *comes out of the house, with*
             MATTHEW. *Both with drinks.*

ZARA   Yes?

GABRIEL   It… it doesn't matter.

MATTHEW   Gabriel. You smoking?

GABRIEL   What? No.

MATTHEW   Not your teacher. You can do what you want.

GABRIEL   No… I…

KATHERINE   Evening.

ZARA   Hello.

GABRIEL   Excuse me.

             GABRIEL *goes.*

KATHERINE   Matthew was just telling me about all the things
             they've found, jewellery, an old wooden box,
             toys.

ZARA   I suppose there've been family after family here.

MATTHEW   Yes, it's had a long history.

KATHERINE   But you're happy, so far, with how it's going?

MATTHEW   Well it's a lot of work, but that's good because
             Cheryl and I, we need the money, and Gabriel
             works hard. Knew nothing about gardens but
             he's a fast learner.

KATHERINE   Sweet boy.

MATTHEW   Dreamer.

KATHERINE   Nothing wrong with that.

MATTHEW   Gardening's looking down, at the ground. Not up at the sky.

ZARA   Maybe he wants more from his life.

MATTHEW   More what? More time? Money? Things aren't so bad for him.

KATHERINE   How's Cheryl?

MATTHEW   Strong, which is a blessing. I keep the bread on the table. Yes, there's a lot of work in the garden but we need the hours. Gabriel works hard. You ladies both alright for a drink?

KATHERINE   I am.

ZARA   Yes.

MATTHEW   Right then. Well you asked me to show you where she was. Done my duty. I'll leave you to catch up.

             He's slightly awkward. He goes.

KATHERINE   Last time we were here together, your mother had done that awful thing.

ZARA   I don't mind now actually. When I visit I come here, and I think it was quite a good idea. Returned him to dust. It's all our fate eventually.

KATHERINE   And what about Anna?

ZARA   Mum says she comes every weekend. Doesn't do much, just sits here.

KATHERINE   Is she alright?

             ZARA *shrugs.*

ZARA   James and her only knew each other a few months. I think we're all surprised she's taken it so hard.

KATHERINE   That's not how love works. Length of time.
             If she feels he was who she was supposed to be
             with, that's that.

ZARA   I wouldn't know.

KATHERINE   Never been in love?

ZARA   Not with a person.

KATHERINE   Huh. What then?

ZARA   I think I was in love with a picture of Beyoncé
             when I was fifteen. I had it framed. It was quite
             weird, but Mum never said anything. Maybe
             she didn't notice. What about you?

KATHERINE   Yes, a few times. But they never returned the
             favour. I chased. It fizzled. Perhaps I was
             scared. I didn't try hard enough.

ZARA   I find that surprising. That it's never worked
             for you.

KATHERINE   Why?

ZARA   Well you're very... you're very attractive. And
             your work is so...

KATHERINE   ?

ZARA   ...my friend has this theory. There are writers
             who when you read their work, see it on the
             stage, whatever, without knowing anything
             about them or what they look like, you feel they
             are writers you know you want to sleep with,
             that you might fall in love with, they're
             seductive and sexy. Iris Murdoch, Emily
             Brontë, Pinter, then there are other writers who
             are brilliant, devastating, funny, whose work
             you love, but you would probably not want to
             get physical with – Dickens, Jane Austen,
             Orwell... you know what I mean?

KATHERINE   I know which category I fall into.

ZARA   No I don't think you do.

             Beat.

KATHERINE   Oh.

              A moment. Then KATHERINE *stands up and moves away.*

              I'm in a very unusual position.

ZARA   What's that?

KATHERINE   I've got to be careful about my friend.

ZARA   What friend?

KATHERINE   Your mother.

ZARA   Why is that unusual?

KATHERINE   Because normally, she forgives my mistakes. She's helped me when I've got into scrapes. Always put a roof over my head when I needed it. Always put me first.

ZARA   I didn't think Mum put anyone first but herself.

KATHERINE   Oh she does. Just very quietly. She's hardly ever done anything for herself. This garden might be the first time.

ZARA   But her business?

KATHERINE   She started that when your father died. To provide for you and James. It's all about you and James to her.

ZARA   She barely touches me. Never hugs me.

KATHERINE   That's manner. Not meaning.

ZARA   So why have you got to be careful?

              Beat.

KATHERINE   Because you're her daughter.

              ZARA *stands. Goes to* KATHERINE.

ZARA   And why have you got to be careful?

              A moment.

KATHERINE   Can you please go and sit back down there, where you were sitting, please.

ZARA   Why?

KATHERINE   You're standing very close to me.

ZARA   I'm not standing particularly close to you.

KATHERINE   Close enough.

                       Beat.

ZARA   For what?

                       Beat.

KATHERINE   Your eyes are bright, no dust and weather.
                       Grown enough to know who you are, what
                       you're doing, young enough not to have fully
                       seen the horror of the world.

ZARA   What do you mean?

KATHERINE   Mortality, loss, the cruelty associated with
                       being alive, when it lands, it changes, most
                       profoundly, one's eyes. Your eyes dim. It means
                       wisdom yes, but inevitably sadness as well.

ZARA   I've lost people. My father. My brother.

KATHERINE   I know. And yet for whatever reason you still
                       have this spark. What shall we call it? Naïveté?
                       Hope?

ZARA   Your eyes are bright too.

KATHERINE   If they are, it's done by avoiding responsibility.
                       Constantly being on the move. No promises.

                       That's why I've got to be careful Zara. Because
                       I think you're very beautiful.

                       A moment.

                       ZARA *touches* KATHERINE.

ZARA   I would do anything for you.

KATHERINE   I know.

                       But I wouldn't do anything for you.

ZARA   I don't mind.

              ZARA touches KATHERINE's face.
              KATHERINE almost flinches.

KATHERINE   I would rather write this than live it.

ZARA   I don't believe that's true.

              ZARA kisses KATHERINE. KATHERINE
              responds. Passionately.

              They stop. Look at each other.

KATHERINE   Oh god.

              KATHERINE takes her hand. Holds it tightly.
              They look at each other.

              GABRIEL comes back in, holding a glass of
              champagne. ZARA quickly lets go of
              KATHERINE's hand, but GABRIEL senses
              he's interrupted something.

GABRIEL   I...

              I brought you a drink.

ZARA   Oh. Thank you. That's kind.

              No one says anything for a moment. GABRIEL
              works out there's something going on between
              them.

GABRIEL   I'm interrupting.

KATHERINE   Not at all.

GABRIEL   Sorry... sorry.

              He goes.

              Another sound – EDWARD and PAUL are
              approaching with ANNA. We hear them
              from off.

EDWARD   – the village is not happy.

PAUL   The village will never be happy.

KATHERINE *looks at* ZARA.

KATHERINE   I can't.

ZARA   You just have.

EDWARD   They tried to have the book day in the school
              playground instead but it was a disaster. There
              was a drizzle, and of course it's nonsense but
              everyone was saying there had never been
              drizzle when it was held here. She wouldn't
              even have the conversation. Said she'd bought
              a garden, not a public park.

              They enter.

              Everyone's said, it won't happen again, unless
              you and Audrey agree to open the garden.

PAUL   She's dead against it I'm afraid.

EDWARD   Many gardens open their doors to hundreds of
              people, and there's not a rumpus. People would
              be respectful.

ANNA   What's she going to do with the garden? Even
              if she makes it exactly as she wants it, what's
              she planning to do with it?

PAUL   Enjoy it. Have friends round. Like this.

ANNA   Themed parties.

PAUL   Yes. Little events I suppose. People we know.

ANNA   What's wrong with people you don't know?

PAUL   More effort.

              ANNA *looks at him.*

              Look don't shoot the messenger here. I'm not in
              charge.

              They enter the garden properly. ANNA *goes
              straight and sits on a small bench by the tree,
              next to* ZARA.

              How are you both? Titans of the literary world.

ZARA	Good.
KATHERINE	Yes, well, thank you.
EDWARD	There's no denying, when it's finished, it'll be beautiful. What are these?
PAUL	Flowers.
EDWARD	Don't you take any interest?
PAUL	None at all. I look at it. Smell it. Sit by it. But that's the extent.
	Not much interest in anything really. I exist, and that's enough.
KATHERINE	What does she see in you?
	ZARA *laughs*.
PAUL	I beg your pardon?
KATHERINE	You're quite unlike Nick.
PAUL	As I've been told many times.
KATHERINE	He was rugged. Sexy. And you're… well I'm not being funny but –
PAUL	As a matter of fact, I know exactly what she sees in me. She's a very busy woman. Running her business. Nick was like her, frantic twenty-four hours a day, and I think once she started to think about someone else, she realised exactly what she needed.
KATHERINE	You?
PAUL	If I was a garden I would be a patio with a few plant pots. Bit of water and a tidy, done for the whole year. Low maintenance.
KATHERINE	And you're happy with that?
PAUL	Oh yes. Edward's the same.
EDWARD	Well no, I have my interests. Birdwatching actually.

ZARA	You're boring Paul. There's no two ways about it.
PAUL	No not boring. That's different. Your mother doesn't find me boring.
ZARA	You don't interrupt. That's all she needs.
EDWARD	Who was the murderer? I lost track.
ZARA	Gabriel.
EDWARD	Ah. Gabriel. I had no idea. Well I had no idea what was going on at all really. Never read an Agatha Christie. They do them on the television as well don't they.
PAUL	They're all the same.
KATHERINE	They're not actually.
EDWARD	Gabriel was the murderer. How did he do it?
PAUL	Didn't you listen at all?
KATHERINE	Strangulation.
EDWARD	You wouldn't think he had the hands.
PAUL	It's all the gardening he's doing now. Matthew's the brain and Gabriel's the brawn. Good for him. Like national service. They should bring that back. Don't you think?
ZARA	You wouldn't have survived.
PAUL	I beg your pardon?
ZARA	If you'd had to do it, you wouldn't have lasted a day.
PAUL	I can build a tent.
ZARA	There's more to it than that –
PAUL	Iron a uniform.
ZARA	Fight? Kill?
PAUL	Kill? Hard to say.
ZARA	Paul you can barely gut a fish.

PAUL   That's cookery, but I'm told by people who
                have killed a person that it very much helps to
                have a sense of detachment and calm. In which
                case I'm ideal.

                Maybe that's why the British have traditionally
                made such good soldiers. Just at the moment
                your conscience should kick in, our British
                attitude answers back. *No*. No mercy. Keep
                calm, carry on. Dead.

                A moment.

EDWARD   Where did it happen?

PAUL   What?

EDWARD   The murder.

PAUL   Oh! You really weren't listening, were you?

ZARA   The billiard room.

EDWARD   *Is* there a billiard room?

PAUL   She's converted the laundry.

EDWARD   It's very complicated isn't it?

ANNA   It's obscene.

PAUL   What?

ANNA   To dress up like this. The 1920s were awful.
                War across the world, women having to fight
                for the vote, racism, rape, murder, child abuse.

PAUL   I don't think you're quite entering into the spirit
                of this evening.

KATHERINE   She's got a point.

ANNA   Most people poor and suffering, no proper
                health care. If we wanted a real 1920s-themed
                evening we should all come as corpses.

PAUL   Well it isn't 1920s it's Agatha Christie and she
                generally had a quota of one corpse per event.

EDWARD   Speaking of corpses, wasn't Geoffrey
           marvellous! I'm surprised he agreed. Didn't
           look like he was breathing.

PAUL   I'm not sure he was. She bribed him with two
           bottles of very good whiskey, and I think he had
           half of one of them before he went down.

ANNA   – I'm just saying I have no idea what she's
           doing! Why she's trying to pretend this whole
           place hasn't moved on? That it's like it was: This
           is the twenty-first century. Things have changed
           for the better. But all these people, descending on
           the old house – they can't wait to dress up as
           masters and servants, as if that was fun.

PAUL   If you think all this Anna why are you here?

           She doesn't answer.

           You like that spot, don't you?

           Beat.

           Always there.

           ZARA *gets up and goes to* ANNA.

ZARA   You want another drink?

ANNA   Yes please.

           They stand and start back for the house.

           AUDREY *emerges from the house laughing.*

AUDREY   Oh girls there you are. I couldn't find anyone
           I liked.

ZARA   Paul's there.

AUDREY   I meant you darling. I like you.

ZARA   And Anna.

AUDREY   Of course Anna, don't be silly. Hello Anna.

ZARA   We're getting a drink.

AUDREY   Try the Twinkles. Not strictly authentic to the period, vodka and champagne, but they go down a treat.

                She moves on. ANNA *and* ZARA *go back inside.*

                AUDREY *comes down into the garden.*

                Here you all are! I was disappointed it was that boy. I mean he shouldn't really have been here at all but Zara insisted on it. I keep asking if she's got a thing for him, and she tells me I'm stupid. Well I might be, but I don't see why that's such an outrageous idea, that she fall for the gardener. It happens in books.

KATHERINE   He's not her type.

AUDREY   Really? She told you?

KATHERINE   She feels sorry for him.

PAUL   Edward's upset about the village events.

AUDREY   Oh I'm sure he is but –

PAUL   It didn't go well apparently.

AUDREY   I thought they were using the school.

EDWARD   There was a drizzle.

AUDREY   Well then there would have been a drizzle here.

EDWARD   If it had rained here that would have added to the magic. There it just made it seem to all the children like another day at school. They left early. We had to cancel the whole thing.

AUDREY   And I got the blame.

EDWARD   Well everyone knew why the venue had changed yes.

AUDREY   You seem to think I have some kind of civic responsibility Edward, to the village. And the truth is I just don't see it like that. I'm employing Krystyna, and Matthew full time now, Gabriel,

	we use the village shop whenever we can, but beyond that –
EDWARD	This is the biggest house in the village –
AUDREY	I would question that.
EDWARD	And the house, and its garden, have been used by the village for decades.
AUDREY	Not Weatherbury. He didn't have the villagers in to stamp over his hard work. He had invited parties, he had evenings where the best gardeners from the south of England would come to admire and discuss his work. He employed a team of gardeners from the village and staff, and that was how he contributed, by providing quite a few of them with an income, and over time, as the house and its garden expands, I'm sure I'll do the same. But it will be a fair deal. Money for services. Anything else is at my discretion.
EDWARD	Alright.
AUDREY	I don't take kindly to bullying and pressure. It's my home.
PAUL	Our home.
AUDREY	Our home precisely.
AUDREY	We get on well Edward.
EDWARD	We do.
AUDREY	And if you feel so strongly about it, your garden is hardly titchy. I'm sure there's enough space there.
EDWARD	My wife and I feel the pond would be too dangerous for children.
AUDREY	I see.
	A moment.
EDWARD	Well, either way tonight is hugely enjoyable. I might head back in and recharge.

AUDREY   Paul's going to go with you.

PAUL   Am I?

AUDREY   Yes.

PAUL   Oh. Right. Alright.

                They turn and leave. AUDREY *and*
                KATHERINE *are left in the garden.*

AUDREY   I read your latest book.

KATHERINE   And did you enjoy it?

AUDREY   I didn't.

KATHERINE   That's a shame.

AUDREY   Did you write it very quickly?

                Beat.

KATHERINE   No.

AUDREY   It felt like it was sneering at people.

KATHERINE   At who?

AUDREY   At people who... Work hard but don't
                necessarily make a lot of money. People who
                don't necessarily have time to understand the
                ins and outs of current affairs.

KATHERINE   Poor people.

AUDREY   Yes, poor people, but also just normal everyday
                people who aren't hugely ambitious but enjoy
                their lives in a dignified and law-abiding way as
                teachers, doctors, shop-keepers, I don't know,
                people who install phone lines. Whatever. There
                was something in the tone which sounded like
                you didn't like these people very much.

KATHERINE   Well I don't. A lot of them. A lot of them I'm
                really fucked off with.

AUDREY   You gave them names like what was it Patricia
                Smallmind? Gary Numb.

KATHERINE   It's a comedy.

AUDREY   It's not exactly subtle.

KATHERINE   It's a satire on the wilfully ignorant people who seem to be full of hate, but whose voice seems to have grown to dominate completely in the last few years. And who are responsible for the shocking result of a completely unnecessary plebicite.

AUDREY   But those people in general are the ones without the power so to satirise them –

KATHERINE   Without the power? That's not true any more. Hungary. The United States. Here? And in time it might create something you really don't want. The rise of something that Weatherbury fought against. That your own son fought against. Fascism. On your doorstep. That's what the book's about. It's not just a satire. It's a warning.

AUDREY   Well it wasn't very funny.

KATHERINE   That's what you look for is it?

AUDREY   In a comedy, yes. It's certainly something to get me from page one to page five hundred and eighty-seven.

Five hundred and eighty-seven pages – that's another thing. There's only three books that need to be that long.

KATHERINE   Shakespeare.

AUDREY   Yes.

KATHERINE   Dickens.

AUDREY   Yes. And? What's the third?

Beat.

KATHERINE   Who's Who?

AUDREY   *The Bible.*

KATHERINE   Well it's selling very well.

AUDREY   The Bible?

KATHERINE   *My book.*

AUDREY   I'm sure. People love to sneer.

KATHERINE   I'm making the point that this feeling is being driven by inequality and resentment.

                There should be tax policies which encourage distribution of wealth.

AUDREY   Yes, alright –

KATHERINE   Everyone should have good quality education, health care, housing –

AUDREY   You're naive Katherine. That's why I love you in my life. I'm head head head, sensible, responsible, wanting facts, practice, preparation. But you're completely heart. You don't need the facts because you *feel* something to be true. And that's wonderful, but I have advised the government on manufacturing policy, on social deprivation, and employment. I know the facts.

KATHERINE   You don't know anyone who earns less than the average salary –

AUDREY   Can we stop please? I know you're being provocative and that's your thing, but I'm not as young as I used to be and I'm looking at the stars and thinking they are beautiful.

                Beat. KATHERINE *looks up.*

KATHERINE   They are.

AUDREY   This garden is all heart, for me. First time in my life. Massive risk.

KATHERINE   Regret it?

AUDREY   Not for a second.

                A moment.

                But I have a problem with Anna.

KATHERINE   Really?

AUDREY   I mean. She wasn't even engaged to James. The evidence of his feelings is a couple of letters, which suggest he wanted to spend his life with her, but... well... who knows? But now since the thing with his ashes, she comes here. Every Saturday.

KATHERINE   To see you.

AUDREY   No *here*, to this garden. She sits under the tree and... reads, all day. Then goes home in the evening. And it means if we want to do work here, in this garden, or make use of it, at the weekend, it's very awkward. She's got no interest in making conversation.

KATHERINE   Well she's stuck on James isn't she?

AUDREY   I don't mean to be cruel. But she's got to find something better to do with her life.

KATHERINE   Talk to her. She clearly loved him. Maybe you can share that.

AUDREY   Grief isn't really something you share. Everyone talks about it like that, but really you go through it on your own. In the nights. When it interrupts your thoughts. Still. Years later. You don't share that. You work it out alone.

KATHERINE   Well she's not working it out at all.

A moment.

AUDREY   I'm considering being cruel to be kind.

KATHERINE   Just be kind.

Beat.

I... er... need to ask you something. Tell you something. Ask you something.

AUDREY   Are you stuck?

KATHERINE   Sorry – It's just. It's awkward.

AUDREY   You can't shock me Katherine. I've seen every
                inch of you at college. All your indiscretions.
                What is it? Have you done something bad?

KATHERINE   No.

AUDREY   You need money?

KATHERINE   It's Zara.

AUDREY   What about her?

KATHERINE   Well... I know this sounds... unlikely.

AUDREY   I have literally never seen you so hesitant.
                Should I call an ambulance? It's like a medical
                condition. What about Zara? Has she said
                something awful? I'll get her to apologise.

KATHERINE   No, please –

AUDREY   She can be very cutting. She's intelligent. And
                that's the unfortunate byproduct. Cruelty. And
                before you say it, yes, much like her mother.

KATHERINE   Aud I'm in love with her.

                A pause.

AUDREY   Why?

KATHERINE   I... I'm sorry?

AUDREY   Why on earth would you be in love with her?

KATHERINE   Audrey...

AUDREY   She's twenty-three. She doesn't have a clue
                how anything works. She's got her father's lack
                of concentration. Her grandmother's
                selfishness. She says the most ridiculous things.

                She's a child.

                My daughter.

                Beat.

KATHERINE   I know.

AUDREY   You've only met her a few times. Here. And
               then your signing that she went to.

KATHERINE   Yes.

AUDREY   And now here again tonight.

               Beat.

               Love? Is that a thing anyone does these days?
               I mean. People sleep with people. They have
               affairs and marriages but I haven't heard of
               anyone 'falling in love' for years.

               Beat.

               Are you lonely?

KATHERINE   No more so than before, no more so than for
               years.

AUDREY   Is it something to do with me? To get back at
               me for something.

KATHERINE   No it's nothing to do with you.

               Beat.

AUDREY   You mustn't tell her. That would be awful. Can
               you imagine some old woman, sorry, some older
               woman coming up to you when you're twenty-
               three and saying they're in love with you. If you
               avoided vomiting on them immediately, it would
               be very awkward, especially if it was your
               mum's best friend. This is like one of those
               stories you see on daytime television.

KATHERINE   She feels the same.

               Beat.

AUDREY   Oh. For Christ's sake it's the books. She's fallen
               in love with the books. Your writing, she's
               being a romantic. She thinks you're some
               blessed creature, touched by a godlike genius to
               write these great works. She flattered you, you
               fell for her, and now she's under your spell,
               with not a thought for how it's actually going to

work, how you're actually going to do things together or have sex. Have you thought about that? How the two of you would have sex?

KATHERINE   Yes.

AUDREY   You – right.

KATHERINE   Quite a lot.

AUDREY   Alright. Well don't. Actually. Maybe you shouldn't.

A moment.

It's absurd.

KATHERINE   I'm sorry.

AUDREY   If I'm honest it disgusts me.

A moment.

I forbid it.

KATHERINE   Aud.

AUDREY   I forbid you Katherine from having anything to do with my daughter. This isn't real. This is unbalanced and unrealistic. There are reasons these kinds of relationships always end badly.

KATHERINE   Not always.

AUDREY   Yes. They always do. An age gap like this. Ten years is possible. Twenty years is highly unlikely. But thirty years is just a physical, biological, scientific impossibility. And if you continue you will come out much the same, but she will be devastated. Her view of the world destroyed.

KATHERINE   I don't agree.

AUDREY   Well how convenient.

Beat. It's quite dark now. There's a rumble of thunder in the distance.

Does our friendship matter to you?

KATHERINE   Of course.

AUDREY   Then don't do it. Put our relationship first, don't go anywhere near her this evening, lock your bedroom door tonight, leave tomorrow and never contact her again. If our friendship means the thirty-six years I think it does, you'll control yourself and do this for me.

KATHERINE   You can't protect her like this. Stop her growing up.

AUDREY   Oh no no no, I want her to grow up. Make mistakes. Live a little. Just not with you. Do I have your word that you'll stay away from her?

It's a crush for her. But for you, it's nostalgia. Remembering when we were just coming up. The potential. But look in the mirror and accept what you see. Alright?

KATHERINE *nods.*

KATHERINE   The head above the heart.

AUDREY   Sometimes it has to be.

ANNA *comes out with a drink. Looks at them –*

ANNA   Katherine, Zara said to tell you that she's in the living room.

ANNA *goes and sits under the tree again.*

A look between AUDREY *and* KATHERINE.

KATHERINE   I might go to bed.

AUDREY   Good idea.

KATHERINE   Goodnight Anna.

ANNA   Night.

KATHERINE   Had a bit too much to drink.

ANNA   Me too. Sleep well.

KATHERINE *smiles and goes inside.*

ANNA *looks at* AUDREY *for the first time this scene, slightly incredulous.*

I was going to go with him to where we first met, Blackfriars Bridge, put some ashes there. Some on his favourite walk, that he used to do with you. Some by the house where you brought him up. I was going to keep some, in a small locket. For me.

But you took all that away.

You're right. I suppose he's in everything here now. The trees, the grass, the plants, whatever they are.

AUDREY   Exactly.

ANNA   But nowhere else. You wanted to claim him and put him in your house. Your garden. Under your protection. Well now he's in the ground this has become my ground. My garden. My plants and my place.

AUDREY   You've clearly had a few.

ANNA   Yeah I have. Seven Twinkles. Why did you let him join the army? Zara said it came out of the blue. She thought you'd talk him round, but you encouraged it. Everyone in his life thought it was a crazy idea but you said you'd be proud of him.

AUDREY   I was proud of him. I still / am.

ANNA   Then he went and got killed in a nasty, nasty way. You know how he died?

AUDREY   Yes.

ANNA   But *exactly* how he died.

AUDREY   I have no desire to hear the gruesome details.

ANNA   I felt I had to. So unlike you I'm living in
              a reality. Living with what really happened.

              Why did you encourage him?

              Beat. Another rumble.

AUDREY   These are my children.

              I don't have to answer to you.

              It's going to rain.

              AUDREY *turns and goes inside, leaving her
              unfinished drink on the small table.*

              Once she's gone, ANNA *gets out headphones
              and puts them in. She presses a button.*

              *We, and she hears, 'Blood Hands' by Royal
              Blood.*

              *She slowly moves to the music, just her head
              at first.*

              It starts to rain.

              She moves more, as the rain comes down.

              *She crying. Mouthing the words to herself. But
              trying to dance through it.*

              *She dances through the plants – getting more
              and more frenzied.*

              It's really raining now.

              *As it gets to the chorus, and the guitars kick in,
              she goes to the tree.*

              Hugs it.

              She kisses it.

              She starts…fucking it.

              Still crying. Screaming.

              AUDREY *appears. She looks at* ANNA, *what
              she's doing.*

ANNA's got her eyes closed, into the moment.

AUDREY goes up to her and then removes the headphones from her ears. The music suddenly stops and we're left with ANNA screaming.

She turns suddenly, to look at AUDREY. Then falls to the ground. Screams again.

Alright. It's alright.

ANNA	It's not. It's *not*.
AUDREY	Just calm down.
ANNA	I've got his baby.
AUDREY	You... Anna?
ANNA	Did you hear what I said? His baby is inside me.
AUDREY	You... You can't. He died two years ago. There's no / way.
ANNA	I'm pregnant!
AUDREY	What?
ANNA	Pregnant with his child!
AUDREY	Come inside and dry off –
ANNA	You're worried people will see.
AUDREY	No. I'm worried about you. Come on.

She pulls away.

ANNA   You're going to be a grandmother! We should be celebrating!

ANNA puts her headphones back in. The music starts again. The rain falls.

She starts dancing again.

AUDREY watches –

ANNA reaches into the ground, finds a hand, pulls, and JAMES appears from the ground, in full military combat uniform.

They dance to the music, mouthing along with the words.

Build noise, movement and rain, and then –

Blackout

End of Act Two.

Interval.

ACT THREE

Early September. The garden is now in full bloom, green, grown, but perhaps slightly too much. Perhaps a little overgrown.

ANNA sits under the oak tree. She's now six months pregnant.

GABRIEL enters. He's got his top off. Six months of work in the garden has had an effect. He's fit, and muscular, carrying a tool for doing the edges of the lawn.

In the background. In the distance, we hear occasional brief snatches of guitar music.

ANNA watches GABRIEL for a while. He hasn't noticed her.

ANNA	Afternoon.
GABRIEL	Oh! Hi.

Beat.

ANNA	She's back today.
GABRIEL	I know.

A moment.

Are you going?

ANNA	Next door? No, it's her birthday.
GABRIEL	I thought perhaps you might, later on. With Zara.
ANNA	We can't. We're celebrating. There's plans.
GABRIEL	Up to you.

A moment.

ANNA	You're looking forward to seeing her? Zara?
GABRIEL	Very much.

ANNA	When does it start?
GABRIEL	What?
ANNA	The festival.
GABRIEL	Soon, but it goes on all evening.
ANNA	Is it fun?
GABRIEL	Yeah, it's like…
	Lanterns. Dancing. Like *A Midsummer Night's Dream*. A real festival – where the normal social order is turned on its head.
ANNA	I can see why she refused permission for that to happen here. Last thing she wants.
	Do you believe there's a one? One person out there, for us all?
GABRIEL	…No.
ANNA	Then you must think it's strange, what I did.
GABRIEL	Don't know what you mean.
ANNA	Oh Gabriel stop lying. I'm fully aware of what you said in the pub –
GABRIEL	I didn't say anything in the pub.
ANNA	– I have my spies, and I realise this is still unusual for people round here. A woman making a decision like this.
	And you'd be right. You'd be flawless in your argument, if it wasn't for the fact that James was my one! My absolute best man and if I'm going to have a child there has been, is, and will be, no one better to be his father. And it's what he wanted, which is why he froze it in the first place. Just in case the worst happens. After she scattered him here. But it made me think you don't know what I meant to him, what he meant to me, and I realised I had to go through with it – the pledge we made to each other. That week,

I made an appointment. Then once it worked…
I couldn't stop coming here. To be with him.
I'll never stop coming here. We'll raise him
together.

GABRIEL   It's a boy?

ANNA   Yes. So what do you think now?

GABRIEL   Don't know.

ANNA   That's your answer?

GABRIEL   How are you feeling?

Any happier?

ANNA   No. But she's being very kind. I'm starting to
see what James meant about her.

You shouldn't have said that in the pub.

GABRIEL   People talk about people.

Beat.

ANNA   The doctor wanted to give me pills.

GABRIEL   Maybe you should think about it.

ANNA   For mood swings.

GABRIEL   Pills can work well.

ANNA   I like my moods.

GABRIEL   Pills give you room to recover.

ANNA   Do you ever hear him? When you're working.

GABRIEL   Who?

ANNA   James. Talking.

GABRIEL   No.

ANNA   Sometimes I see him too.

GABRIEL   You think you see him.

ANNA   Tell that to your mates in the pub. Or put it in
one of your stories. When do you start your
course? Must be soon right? New term.

GABRIEL   Well... I...

He's about to answer when CHERYL *enters,*
with a rug that she empties the crumbs out of.

CHERYL   You must be keen to get next door.

GABRIEL   Yeah. In a bit.

CHERYL   Your friends going?

GABRIEL   Most of them aren't around now. Uni.

CHERYL *looks around then sits down, in the*
sun. Takes a moment.

CHERYL   Matthew and I will be. We love it, and he's
good mates with Jeff Lesley who's on later.
Last year, they played on the steps, those steps
over there – picnic blankets, the whole village
out listening. It wasn't the notes that were
magical, it was the silences in between.
Could've heard a pin drop. Just shivers down
the spine. Seems a long time ago all that, now.

Beat.

Be different this year. Smaller. But it's good of
Edward. And if the weather holds.

Matthew used to sing. Long time ago.

How about you? You going?

GABRIEL   They have to stay here, for when she gets back.

CHERYL   Well she doesn't *have* to.

ANNA   I made her a cake.

CHERYL   That's yours? It looks very nice.

ANNA   Thanks.

CHERYL   How are you?

ANNA   Why does everyone keep asking me that?

GABRIEL	Because you look ill.
	A moment.
	I should get on.
	GABRIEL *leaves.*
ANNA	It's sponge. I made the jam from the strawberries in the garden.
CHERYL	Very enterprising.
ANNA	She says one day there'll be a whole vegetable garden round the side. She says it'll be able to sustain the house for the year.
CHERYL	Well... we'll see.
ANNA	What?
CHERYL	Rumours.
ANNA	What rumours?
CHERYL	Just that. No point repeating.
	AUDREY *enters. She looks a little tired.*
AUDREY	Oh I've missed this!
	CHERYL *stands up.*
CHERYL	I was just... I'd only just... *sat down.*
AUDREY	It's fine Cheryl.
ANNA	How was London?
AUDREY	Oh. Two days was enough. Best thing we did, getting out of it. London's a workplace, not a home. So easy to see that now.
ANNA	I agree.
AUDREY	You? No. I only feel that because I'm old, but you must miss the excitement of it, don't you?
ANNA	London's just about money now.

AUDREY	Well, Zara will be here shortly. Someone to play with.
CHERYL	I believe her room's ready.
AUDREY	We'll have the cake out here. Anna I assume there's a cake?
ANNA	Wait and see.
AUDREY	Don't be obtuse, I'm tired, had a long day and I need to make plans, is there a cake or not?
ANNA	Yes. I made it.
AUDREY	Right then, well perhaps bring it out here, we'll have tea. You made it? Made it yourself?
ANNA	Yes.
AUDREY	And it's…
ANNA	What?
AUDREY	It's alright is it? It looks like a cake?

Some music from next door.

They listen, then it stops again. AUDREY *rolls her eyes.*

	Uh! We'll just have to ignore that I suppose. Why is it starting and stopping?
CHERYL	Sound check.
AUDREY	I thought it was acoustic guitars.
CHERYL	No, all sorts, there's a stage, microphones.
AUDREY	In Edward's garden. Why? It's tiny.
ANNA	Apparently it's a lot of fun.
AUDREY	I'm sorry?
ANNA	The festival. I actually thought, maybe after tea, we could all go.
AUDREY	There? No. I've got plans for us this evening. Zara particularly. Been looking forward to it. I haven't seen her for months, I don't want her

disappearing. I've pictured this afternoon. This evening. My birthday, in this wonderful garden. With my family around me. I have a picture in my head.

Another snatch of music.

The sound isn't ideal, but at least let me have the picture.

ANNA   Bet this wasn't in the picture.

              AUDREY *looks at her pregnant tummy.*

AUDREY   As a matter of fact it was. Might not be what we all imagined, but I don't deny facts.

              A moment.

CHERYL   Excuse me. I better get on. Lots to do.

              CHERYL *goes.*

              AUDREY *rolls her eyes.*

AUDREY   Honestly I'd pay an extra pound an hour to lose the atmosphere.

              A moment.

              There's something I wanted to talk to you about. It's very awkward but you mentioned a few days ago you were looking to give up your flat.

ANNA   Yes.

AUDREY   Well that confused me, and I wondered what your plan was? With this child on the way, where are you intending to live?

ANNA   I... when you put me to bed that night, you said it was alright and that you would look after me as long as I needed. That I could stay here, with James, as long as that was useful.

AUDREY   Yes but –

ANNA   And it's been perfect. I love it. I walk along the Croft every morning, by the fields. I picked plums from the bush, made a crumble and ate it

all, yesterday, while you were away. I don't
want to go back.

AUDREY   Your work –

ANNA   I'm signed off. You and Paul have been so kind
– And in London, working, every day, in
marketing, just to pay the rent. I forgot what life
was about – I'm even making friends.

AUDREY   Really?

ANNA   Yes.

AUDREY   Because you spend so much time in this
garden –

ANNA   What better place for a child to grow up? I know
we haven't spoken about it, but I was intending
to. And I thought that of course you'd want your
own grandchild under your roof.

A moment.

AUDREY   There's the issue of independence.

ANNA   And if I'm living here then there's no point
in continuing to pay rent on a London flat.
So I thought if I let it go...

AUDREY   Anna... Paul and I have also had a lovely time
with you here. I'm pleased that it's gone some
way to getting you back on your feet. But... to
stay here in the long term, is something quite
different.

ANNA   I know, I should have mentioned it before now,
but I was worried what you might say.

AUDREY   I don't believe it's good for us, as grandparents
to this child, to take away your independence.

ANNA   What do you mean?

AUDREY   At the moment you have a flat of your own,
a life of your own, and that's what you need to
rely on – to build up as you become a mother.
Not to fall back on us. To live our life.

ANNA	I'm not leaving.
AUDREY	Look –
ANNA	You promised.

ANNA stares at her.

AUDREY	I know it's difficult.
ANNA	That's not an answer.

Just words to fill the silence.

A moment. AUDREY resolute.

I need to finish the icing.

She goes.

A moment – AUDREY on her own. She breathes, stressed.

She practices her 'calming' exercises in her head.

Then she goes to the plants. Picks a leaf off and smells it, trying to calm herself down.

CHERYL comes back in with a tray of tea things. She looks tired.

AUDREY	Honestly Cheryl, if you want to sit down for a moment…
CHERYL	I'm fine.
AUDREY	You're not. Please…

CHERYL does stop for a second. A little irritated. Takes a moment.

Cheryl, you're not happy with me.

I can't have awkwardness in my own home.

Tell me.

CHERYL	You said I was slow.
AUDREY	No. I… who told you that?

CHERYL   Zara told Gabriel. He told Matthew.

AUDREY   Well Gabriel shouldn't be talking about things
                that don't concern him.

                Beat.

                Yes, I suppose I did feel that the size of the
                house, with the standard I required was too
                much for you. And then you got ill and the
                choice was out of our hands wasn't it really?
                Now it's worked out for the best.

CHERYL   Not the same hours.

AUDREY   No but –

CHERYL   Matthew can't keep working like he is. He's not
                well either.

AUDREY   What do you mean?

                She doesn't say.

                None of my business. Sorry.

CHERYL   Point is, I'll take any extra hours you can give.

AUDREY   Well that's up to Krystyna isn't it? I just require
                that the house is clean.

CHERYL   I thought you asked –

AUDREY   I asked her to consider you for some work here
                yes, and she clearly did, so that's good.

CHERYL   She takes a cut.

AUDREY   Well… she's managing it, isn't she?

                KRYSTYNA *appears.*

KRYSTYNA   Did you finish the dining room?

CHERYL   Nearly.

KRYSTYNA   Everything else is done.

CHERYL   Do you have a problem with me?

AUDREY   Cheryl...

KRYSTYNA   I... I work with you. Mrs Walters asked me to
              take you on and I said yes, that's fine.

CHERYL   You're rude to me.

KRYSTYNA   I don't really know you. Sorry –

AUDREY   Krystyna it's alright –

CHERYL   You don't have a sense of humour.

KRYSTYNA   I'm at work.

AUDREY   Maybe this is a cultural thing.

KRYSTYNA   No.

CHERYL   No it isn't.

KRYSTYNA   You think I took your job.

CHERYL   You did take / my job.

KRYSTYNA   Mrs Walters gave the work to me. That's up
              to her.

CHERYL   I've not been well.

KRYSTYNA   I know and / I'm sorry about that.

CHERYL   I'd been here twenty years.

AUDREY   And you're still here.

CHERYL   Not like I was.

              A moment.

KRYSTYNA   I don't know what to say.

AUDREY   It's alright Krystyna, thank you.

KRYSTYNA   I'll finish up in the kitchen, then I'll go.

AUDREY   Thank you.

              She goes.

CHERYL   I shouldn't have said all that.

              Beat.

AUDREY   What's wrong with Matthew?

CHERYL   I can't tell you.

AUDREY   Please.

CHERYL   He's proud.

           MATTHEW *enters*.

MATTHEW   Chatting on the job.

CHERYL   You chat on the job.

MATTHEW   What I do is different. Gardening's an art.

CHERYL   Cleaning's a science.

AUDREY   How's the holly?

MATTHEW   Nearly gone.

AUDREY   And the box?

MATTHEW   Coming Thursday. I won't be here but Gabriel knows what to do.

AUDREY   Gabriel doesn't talk to me. He used to say hello at least, but now he just nods. Have I done something wrong?

MATTHEW   He's a quiet lad. In his own world. I'll tell him to be polite.

AUDREY   ...No. Don't. It's fine.

MATTHEW   Up to you. Well I'm heading off now. Had an early start. Gabriel will stay until four probably. He's doing the borders. You sure you don't want extra hours now, or tomorrow?

AUDREY   No thank you. I think we're fine.

MATTHEW   Not as finished as I'd like. There's work to be done in here.

AUDREY   It's quite alright. Go home.

MATTHEW   Your garden Mrs Walters. When are you finished?

CHERYL	Shortly.
MATTHEW	Box is coming on Thursday.
CHERYL	You said.
MATTHEW	I… right then. See you tomorrow.

He goes.

AUDREY	There's nothing I should know?
CHERYL	He loves this place. It's his whole life.

He stays up at night reading the documents, going over photographs.

When you cut down the hours it wasn't the money he missed. He just wasn't sure you could get what you wanted in the time.

AUDREY   I thought we should pace ourselves. We've made good progress this year. We can enjoy it, do a little less.

CHERYL   Right.

A moment.

AUDREY   Has he seen anyone?

CHERYL   Not yet.

AUDREY   The sooner the better. There's pills.

CHERYL   Nothing worse than unsolicited advice Mrs Walters.

He'd be nothing without his pride. His dignity.

AUDREY   Well that I understand.

Beat.

Cheryl, Zara's on her way. Be here any minute. Could you ask Krystyna to bring us some tea out?

CHERYL   I don't mind doing it.

AUDREY   Well… either way.

            She goes off.

            AUDREY *stands for a moment. She's stressed,
            but attempts to stay calm.*

            'A constant process. One is always tending,
            pruning, encouraging and evolving. Never still,
            never ending, always in flux.

            Goes to a flower. Looks at it. Stares at it. PAUL
            enters, unseen at first.

            But still one can enjoy the resting beauty of
            a certain summer day. When all of nature takes
            a breath, and in a second stops –

            *For a second after the word stops, there is no
            sound at all. Then –*

            – waiting there to be beheld.'

PAUL   Happy birthday.

            She doesn't look round.

AUDREY   I thought when we got here I could relax. But
            it's like a warzone.

PAUL   Look.

            She looks. PAUL *is holding a small present.*

AUDREY   Should I open it?

PAUL   You should.

            She does. It's an old trowel.

            It was Weatherbury's. Took quite a bit of
            tracking down. To a collector in the States. I got
            in contact. Made him an offer. Reasonable chap.

AUDREY   This was it?

PAUL   Certainly one of them, and we *think* it's
            probably the one you see in the photos, the one
            he refers to in his diary, just because the
            handle's been replaced at some point.

AUDREY   I… had no idea.

PAUL   This means a lot to you.

AUDREY   It does.

A moment. PAUL *sits.*

PAUL   Have you had a chance to think about it all?

AUDREY   Paul we've only just got home.

PAUL   Of course.

Beat.

Absolutely.

Beat.

It's just they took me aside after dinner last night. Gave me a wonderful brandy. Didn't ask for it. They hoped I might have a word.

AUDREY   You? About what?

PAUL   There were things they were nervous to say, to your face.

AUDREY   What things?

PAUL   Without you, they're struggling.

AUDREY   I'm there for the key decisions.

PAUL   They feel your attention isn't what it was.

AUDREY   They're right, it's not. My attention is here. They should be able to deal with this –

PAUL   Apparently they can't. Everything's changed this year, hasn't it, I suppose. Rocky road.

AUDREY   You just want to go back to London. To your galleries, your concerts. Desperate to go back to your kind of people.

PAUL   Tremendously unfair. I want what you want.

AUDREY   I want to do this.

PAUL   Alright then.

AUDREY   Look what we've achieved. Isn't it magnificent?

PAUL   It's wonderful.

AUDREY   One sits here, looks out, and you get just
            a glimpse of what this place was. What it felt
            like. Something utterly unique.

            Beat.

PAUL   The only thing is… it's not real. Is it? It's
            a choice, to live in the past.

AUDREY   But if we do it, it won't be the past, it'll be now.
            It'll be new and full of opportunity. It can be
            more than it was with Weatherbury. Expand it,
            new plants, new ideas. This is our little piece of
            the world, and we're allowed to do with it,
            exactly as we like.

            Yes?

            There are problems, I admit but we'll find
            a solution. We need optimism. Fighting talk.
            More hours. Harder work. That's the way
            forward. Spirit! We can do this. Yes? Together.
            We'll fix the business and we'll keep this whole
            thing expanding, growing. I know we can.
            Just… let me have my birthday today. I'll come
            up with a solution, I will. But *tomorrow*.

            Beat.

PAUL   It would certainly be a shame not to use the
            trowel.

            She smiles.

AUDREY   Where would I be without you?

PAUL   In exactly the same place, I think. I just count
            myself lucky to be along for the ride.

            A moment.

AUDREY   I tried to speak to Anna.

PAUL   How did she take it?

AUDREY   She didn't.

              KATHERINE *enters. She looks a little tired,
              defensive. She has two flowers in her hair.*

KATHERINE   Hello.

AUDREY   You... Oh.

KATHERINE   Happy birthday.

AUDREY   I didn't... What are you doing here? I didn't
              think... Are you with Zara?

KATHERINE   I'm afraid Zara's not coming.

AUDREY   Yes she is... she's getting the train.

KATHERINE   I was at Paddington to see her off and she...
              didn't feel well. We... she felt that I should
              come instead. To give you her present. Wish
              you happy birthday, from both of us.

              Here.

              *She holds out a small box. Then leaves it on
              the table.*

              And now I have, I can turn straight back round
              and back to London if you want, but we felt one
              of us should be here.

AUDREY   Why didn't she come?

KATHERINE   She didn't feel well.

AUDREY   She was fine on the phone.

KATHERINE   Well sometimes these things happen quickly
              don't they? You'll have to take my word.

              Beat.

AUDREY   And you two...

PAUL   Hello Katherine.

KATHERINE   Hi Paul. You alright?

PAUL   Yes thanks.

KATHERINE   Yes? Us two...?

AUDREY   You're still...

KATHERINE   She's living in my house yes Aud you know
                that, she's been there weeks.

                Beat.

AUDREY   I'm sorry but I'm going to need a better
                explanation than she wasn't feeling well. I've
                got my mobile, she could have called at any
                point. I could call her.

KATHERINE   She won't answer.

AUDREY   What's going on?

KATHERINE   I told her I'd just say she wasn't feeling well.

AUDREY   You need to work on your excuses, it's a vital
                part of being a functioning couple, having
                believable excuses for each other, isn't it Paul?

PAUL   Yes, it is.

AUDREY   So?

                Beat.

KATHERINE   She doesn't like it here. She says the people are
                small-minded. She finds the garden, this
                garden, with the association with James, she
                says she finds it morbid, and awful. And she
                hates the tension between you and Anna.

AUDREY   There isn't any tension.

PAUL   Actually they're getting on rather well at the
                moment.

AUDREY   What does she mean the people are
                small-minded?

KATHERINE   Well...

AUDREY   The people round here might not be at the
                cutting edge of whatever fashion gives her

a sense of worth, but they're better than the friends she tends to make.

KATHERINE   I'm just relaying what she said at the station. I didn't see it coming either, but she very much freaked out.

AUDREY   Surely even if she hated it here, she'd know how much it would mean to see me on my birthday.

A moment.

KATHERINE   Well. I've delivered my message, and more than I intended. Would you like me to stay, or turn round and leave. I'd understand either way.

AUDREY *looks at her.*

AUDREY   You look ridiculous.

KATHERINE   I wanted to be celebratory. You're only fifty-five once. And the last birthday of yours I got to was when you were twenty-seven. Had them then too. So I thought I'd make an effort. Bought them in the station. Couple in my hair.

CHERYL *brings out the tea in a pot, some cups, milk, sugar, some biscuits. She also moves some chairs into the right place.*

This is from her. Happy birthday.

AUDREY   Right. Thank you.

KATHERINE   Hello Cheryl.

CHERYL   Oh.

Hello.

CHERYL *goes.* AUDREY *opens the present. It's a necklace.*

PAUL   Very nice.

AUDREY   You bought this.

KATHERINE   No we both –

AUDREY	There's absolutely no possibility that she would choose a necklace, and it's even less likely, even if she did, that it would suit me.
KATHERINE	I helped.
AUDREY	She said you were encouraging her to write.
KATHERINE	Yes, and I've put her in touch with a few people who have read some sections, and been encouraging.
AUDREY	Is she really up to that? Is it good?
KATHERINE	Very promising.
AUDREY	I never had her down as someone creative like that.
KATHERINE	Well she is.
	CHERYL *brings the cake out. It's an iced sponge with a '55' on the top.*
CHERYL	Here we are.
PAUL	Look at that! Wonderful.
KATHERINE	Why does it say 'SS'?
AUDREY	I suspect it's supposed to be fifty-five. Anna made it. Cheryl where is Anna?
CHERYL	She said I should bring it out, make a start, light the candles.
AUDREY	But where is she?
CHERYL	She was heading upstairs.
AUDREY	Oh Paul go and get her, we're not doing this without her. I hope she's not going into a mood because of what we spoke about. Would you?
PAUL	With pleasure.
	PAUL *goes.*
KATHERINE	What did you speak about?
AUDREY	Nothing.

Another blast of music.

KATHERINE   What's that?

AUDREY   Every year the village holds its own music
            festival apparently. And I'm told, like
            everything else, it traditionally happened in my
            back garden. Well they've got the message so
            they didn't even ask me now. Edward's having
            it in his garden instead. They had to reduce the
            size of it, I understand, but clearly not the
            volume.

KATHERINE   The garden has grown.

AUDREY   Yes. We've laid out the projects for next year.
            You can see it's going to take a while, but even
            from what we've achieved in here, you can see
            the potential.

            GABRIEL *enters. He's now wearing clothes for
            the festival. He's got a can of beer, open.*

            Gabriel! I thought you'd finished for the day.

GABRIEL   I... have. Oh. Hi.

KATHERINE   Hello.

GABRIEL   How are you?

KATHERINE   I'm well. Thank you.

GABRIEL   Is Zara here?

KATHERINE   Zara couldn't make it.

GABRIEL   She... I thought...

KATHERINE   She wasn't well.

GABRIEL   Right. She's... I emailed her, and she said she
            was coming.

KATHERINE   I'm afraid not.

GABRIEL   And you and her, you're still...

            An awkward moment.

KATHERINE   Still?

GABRIEL   Together?

KATHERINE   Yes we are.

Beat.

AUDREY   Have you been at the festival?

GABRIEL   Yes.

AUDREY   How is it?

GABRIEL   Good. Just starting. Is Anna ready?

AUDREY   What?

GABRIEL   She just messaged. Said she wanted to come. Asked me to come and get her.

AUDREY   She's with me this afternoon.

GABRIEL   Okay but she messaged.

A moment.

AUDREY   She's in the house.

GABRIEL   Right.

GABRIEL *looks at them, then goes.*

AUDREY   Another one gone. I hope you like cake Katherine.

CHERYL   Shall I light the candles?

AUDREY   No. Thank you Cheryl, we'll manage. If you need to go home, now would be a good time.

CHERYL   I don't mind.

AUDREY   Really. We're fine.

CHERYL   Alright.

She goes. A moment.

AUDREY   Wait for Paul to come back I suppose.

Another burst of music

I checked with the council, but there's nothing
I can do. No right to peace and quiet. That one
can go out in your garden and have it as you
want it to be. Even on your birthday.

Beat.

They hate me in the village. They have names
for me.

But I'll win them round. When the garden's
complete. And a success. Attracting high-profile
visitors, and this village is back on the map.
When I'm dead and gone and the National Trust
take it over, and tourists flock in, and the village
thrives, I will be thanked.

Pause.

They hated Weatherbury too. By all accounts he
had four friends, all other gardeners. He didn't
socialise with anyone locally, or the staff. He
just focused his energies on the garden, and if
he hadn't, we wouldn't have the model for all
English gardens in the future. The genius and
the glory.

Still. I knew this wasn't going to be easy. Some
things are worth the ignominy. The trouble.
What this country was built on.

Strong ideas.

Principles, Katherine.

Beat.

There's a little tea room, by the shop. I'd love
to go and have a coffee sometimes. But I can't.

Beat.

KATHERINE   It's not nice to be hated.

To be talked about.

A moment.

AUDREY   Zara's not a writer. Why are you lying to her?

KATHERINE   Her writing's raw, needs shaping but –

AUDREY   No.

KATHERINE   – Audrey really it's –

AUDREY   She's your prey. You flatter her so she stays
              with you. Katherine I begged, I stood here in
              this garden and said if our friendship means
              anything you should leave her alone. And you
              promised you would. Next thing I know you
              and her are living together.

KATHERINE   We're in love.

AUDREY   She might be but you should know better. I lie
              in bed just thinking about what you're doing to
              my daughter. I think about it all the time.

KATHERINE   We used to lie in bed together.

AUDREY   I beg your pardon.

KATHERINE   Have you forgotten? You and I. We'd talk
              through the night.

AUDREY   Talk yes, but we never –

KATHERINE   What?

AUDREY   I never had feelings for you.

KATHERINE   I did.

AUDREY   What?

KATHERINE   I had feelings for you at the time. But then…

AUDREY   What?

KATHERINE   I got to know you.

              Beat.

AUDREY   You were always dangerous.

              Beat.

This is a betrayal. And I'd love to say it comes as a surprise but I learnt when we were twenty-one. When the chips were down with me, no money, my family in another country, dumped by my boyfriend, I called you up and said I needed help and you made all sorts of promises, but you never actually came, you never looked after me.

KATHERINE   I had a life of my own –

AUDREY   My son dies and you don't visit. You send an email but you don't write a letter like everyone else.

KATHERINE   I...

AUDREY   What?

KATHERINE   I felt it very deeply.

AUDREY   In your email you said you'd be there, you said you'd keep checking in with me, you said if there was anything you could do just to let me know. That you were there for me.

KATHERINE   And I meant it.

AUDREY   But you weren't. There.

You never checked in with me.

KATHERINE   I didn't know what to say.

AUDREY   But yet you managed five hundred and eighty-seven pages on people that don't exist.

A moment.

KATHERINE   I know everything about you, and your family, I keep up, I ask you questions every time we meet, but what do you really know about me? About things that have happened to me?

AUDREY   What is there to know?

KATHERINE   Exactly. You didn't even know people bought my books. Have I fallen in love before? What about *my* family?

AUDREY   You don't have a family.

KATHERINE   You're sure about that? Every conversation we
              have I come away from feeling I'm a hundred
              per cent up to date on your life, and that you're
              none-the-wiser on mine because you don't ask.

AUDREY   You tell me stories.

KATHERINE   I entertain you because if I don't you start
              thinking about something else.

AUDREY   Oh nonsense –

KATHERINE   – because I don't have children like one is
              supposed to. Don't live in one place, I don't like
              men. I don't live a life that you understand or
              approve of, so you just put me in a generally
              'eccentric' place, and move on. We're not
              friends. I'm a supporting character in your story.

AUDREY   So why do you keep coming back?

KATHERINE   I asked myself that before I got on the train
              today and you know what I believe is the
              reason?

AUDREY   Enlighten me.

KATHERINE   I think I feel I owe you something. You looked
              after me at university. I'm aware I've let you
              down and I think I feel guilty.

              But since meeting Zara, that's gone. Because
              she does ask me about myself. She knows more
              about me after four months than you do in
              thirty years, and you're wrong, we're going to
              stay together for a very long time, and you're
              twice wrong because she has genuine talent and
              it *will* be recognised. It's a shame it hasn't been
              by you.

AUDREY   I know my daughter.

KATHERINE   You really don't Aud.

              A moment.

AUDREY   Your judgement is impaired by lust. You'll ruin her. So Katherine I'm going to make this very clear to you. Either you let her go, or I will arrange a profile piece in the *Sunday Times Magazine* where I go into every detail of this. My daughter's infatuation with this older novelist. How you appeared to groom her, then lured her into your home and stopped her talking to me. I will destroy your reputation and career, unless you stop.

KATHERINE   You don't get to make those decisions for her –

AUDREY   I do.

KATHERINE   – because she's an adult.

AUDREY   I do.

KATHERINE   She's allowed to make her own choice.

AUDREY   No she isn't I'm her mother and contrary to popular belief amongst daughters mothers actually do continue to know what's best till they die. Not that you would understand that.

KATHERINE   Did I want children, and couldn't have them?
Have I ever been pregnant?
What's my brother's name?
Are my parents alive?
When did I come out?
What other friends do I have?

AUDREY   *You're never here.*

KATHERINE   *You wonder why?*

    Do your article. Because when they call me up and ask me about my friend Audrey Walters I'll say I don't know what she's talking about, she's not my friend, she doesn't know me at all.

    PAUL *comes back in.*

PAUL   Anna's going.

AUDREY   We know. To the festival. Now come and sing me happy birthday.

PAUL   No. Properly going. She's packed a bag. I tried
              to stop her, but she's standing in the hall right
              now and she says if you don't come in there
              this minute and reassure her that she can stay
              here, she's going to the festival with Gabriel,
              going to get drunk, and never come back. That
              you'd never see your grandchild again.

AUDREY   I won't be threatened.

              This minute?

PAUL   Yes.

              AUDREY sighs.

AUDREY   One minute?

PAUL   Yes. What did you say to her?

              Twenty seconds pass.

              You're not going to try to stop her?

AUDREY   Empty threats.

              Twenty seconds pass.

KATHERINE   Principle's fine Audrey but you'll end up alone.

              Another twenty seconds. Then it's done.

AUDREY   There.

              Sit down Paul.

              He does.

              She won't drink, she's not stupid. She'll just go,
              and calm down, and work out I'm right. She
              can't live here her whole life.

KATHERINE   You said she had to leave?

AUDREY   She's obsessed with this garden. It isn't healthy.

KATHERINE   Coming from you.

AUDREY   Not the plants. My son.

KATHERINE   What are you doing with your life Audrey?

AUDREY   I'm sticking to a set of values. Holding the line.
Or we'd have chaos. We'd lose what men died
to protect. And if I'm the only one. If that
means I'm on my own then so be it. You look
like you want to leave.

KATHERINE   Desperately.

AUDREY   Then go, and get on the train and when you get
back to the house, to my daughter, pack her
bags and say it's finished. Throw her out on the
step and tell her to *get* home.

A moment.

KATHERINE   And you wonder why she didn't come.

*KATHERINE looks at her for a moment, then
goes.*

Bye Paul.

PAUL   Goodbye.

She leaves.

A moment.

PAUL stands, rather confused.

He lights the candles.

Just us then.

He sings.

Happy birthday to you.

Happy birthday to you.

Happy birthday dear Audrey.

He doesn't finish.

A moment.

I'm so completely in love with you.

The music from next door starts playing at full volume.

The candles burn down and stop.

As they sit there, the plants turn brown.

The leaves die and fall to the ground.

End of Act Three.

ACT FOUR

Mid-November. The garden has died away. Not pruned back or left to bed properly. The plants have died, and fallen, rotted. Much of the grass has been trampled. There's a lot of bare soil again. A lot of mud.

An old washing machine has been left there. And some curtain rails.

One of the main branches of the tree has gone.

ZARA enters, also in a coat. She looks older. Worn out. She's holding a cup of tea. She's lower energy now, then when we last saw her. Her eyes have maybe lost that brightness.

KRYSTYNA comes out, in her coat, tidying up.

ZARA turns, sees her, and smiles.

ZARA	Can I ask you a question?
KRYSTYNA	Of course.
ZARA	What's it like? Cleaning.
	KRYSTYNA looks at her.
KRYSTYNA	It is sometimes about scrubbing other people's shit off toilet bowls. It is sometimes about being on your hands and knees and working hard. But with the right tools, it's not so difficult.
ZARA	Is it what you want to do?
KRYSTYNA	No. I am not a cleaner. I have a plan.
ZARA	What plan?
KRYSTYNA	My boyfriend is in Poland now, and doing well. I will join him in two months and we'll work together. We think in a year, we'll buy a house.

ZARA	You like Poland?
KRYSTYNA	Yes. I mean. It's a place.
ZARA	Maybe I'll move to Poland.
KRYSTYNA	You should. It's very beautiful. Well, some of it.
	I heard what you did. Your mother told me. I was the only person here when she got off the phone and I think she wanted to tell someone so she told me.
ZARA	I feel like dying.
KRYSTYNA	It's nothing.
ZARA	It was in the papers.
KRYSTYNA	I saw. But everyone will forget.
ZARA	They won't.
KRYSTYNA	They will. They don't know who you are really. They don't care that much.
ZARA	I don't know who I am.
KRYSTYNA	It's not important to know who you are. Just what you want to do. What do you want to do today?
ZARA	Hide.
KRYSTYNA	Okay. Then hide.
	AUDREY *enters, wearing a coat and with a holdall. She's with* EDWARD.
	I'm leaving now.
AUDREY	Krystyna. Thank you. Do stay in touch.
KRYSTYNA	I will.
AUDREY	I've enjoyed our conversations. I have this feeling that you… you'll do very well.
KRYSTYNA	Yes. I think so too.
	She goes.
	AUDREY *looks around. Takes in the air.*

ZARA   She's amazing.

AUDREY   She is.

           Edward, thank you for all you've done. I'm so
           sorry for the inconvenience.

EDWARD   How long will they be building?

AUDREY   Eight months.

EDWARD   Do you think… will it… look the same?

AUDREY   You've seen the plans.

EDWARD   Yes, but it's so hard to tell. We made our
           objections, but they fell on deaf ears. I understand
           there's a push for more housing but it's just not
           what this place was meant to be. Is it?

           I almost wonder if they're so keen on making it
           into flats, if they would do better to pull the
           whole thing down and start again.

           You do have to go?

AUDREY   Yes.

EDWARD   And was there really no other buyer?

AUDREY   Not at a reasonable price.

EDWARD   Nothing left, in the end, is there, but money?

           Always money.

AUDREY   Thank you.

EDWARD   What for?

AUDREY   You've always been kind.

EDWARD   Oh. Well. I hope so.

           Anyway. Goodbye. We'll make the best of it.

           We always do.

           New neighbours. Lots of them. Got to help
           business at the shop I suppose…

           He goes. A moment.

ZARA   Sorry Mum.

AUDREY   It's alright.

ZARA   I love you.

AUDREY   You too.

              PAUL *enters, with some car keys.*

PAUL   They're nearly finished.

ZARA   That was quick.

PAUL   Well you saw how many of them there were.
              Ruthless. That's why they're so fast I suppose.
              No sentiment. They just scoop it into boxes and
              gone. And thank goodness. Not long now. Did
              you check the bedroom.

AUDREY   Yes. I think so.

ZARA   When does it happen?

PAUL   In an hour. Well. Fifty minutes. Completion at
              1 p.m. All being well.

              You want me to take that? Put it in the car.

AUDREY   What?

PAUL   Your bag?

AUDREY   Oh. Thank you.

PAUL   Can you do a last check downstairs? That
              we've got everything?

AUDREY   Of course.

              PAUL *goes, taking* AUDREY*'s bag.*

              A moment.

              Sorry this is all happening. Last thing you want,
              you need stability.

ZARA   We'll have it in a couple of days. Back on home
              turf. Not the same house but all our old friends,
              the old places. It'll be so good to be back.

AUDREY	Renting.
ZARA	Only till you find the right place.

AUDREY *looks at the garden. She touches the tree.*

AUDREY	I dreamt of dying in this garden. An old woman, surrounded by grandchildren, great-grandchildren, the sunlight on my face. I'd just go, and no one would realise for a while. That's how peaceful it would be. And now... well...
ZARA	You're a long way off that.
AUDREY	No. I'm not. Not really.

A moment.

Have you heard anything from her?

ZARA	No.
AUDREY	Why did you do it?
ZARA	She wouldn't return my calls. My emails. Texts. And I had to speak to her.
AUDREY	Why?
ZARA	It didn't make sense. We were close. Everything was good. And then suddenly she went cold.
AUDREY	She gets scared of stability. Relationships.
ZARA	But I was different.
AUDREY	She didn't talk to you about it?
ZARA	As the weeks went past, I realised the reason she didn't want me contacting her was that I'm an embarrassment. The number of important people in the literary world I met as her girlfriend...

I must've looked so stupid. I'll always be that idiot girl on her arm.

AUDREY   Until you do something more important.

ZARA   Not very likely. My writing's childish. When they thought I was her girlfriend, they were all complimentary – the agents, publishers. Now the word's got out it's over. They'll probably not return my calls even.

Especially after what I did.

AUDREY   Tell me.

ZARA   You know.

AUDREY   I know it was coffee.

ZARA   Well that's it really. She was halfway through a reading, and I walked to the front and just threw this large cup of coffee over her, and shouted that she was the opposite of everything she professed. She was cruel, and she hated women, she hated people, she was loathsome and selfish I shouted and shouted – I was crying – I had to be led away…

It was in the news the next day. They called me an ex-lover. 'Lover'. That tone they use when it's the same sex. Like arguments and violence is inevitable.

You put my name into Google, pictures come up of me shouting on that day. The whole story. Can't remove it. That's me forever. I look mentally ill.

Maybe I am.

AUDREY   You're not ill. Just young.

Beat.

So what's happening with your book?

ZARA   I've sent it to a couple of agents I met but –

AUDREY   Good. At least they know who you are now.

You've got contacts. Exploit them.

A moment.

ZARA   You didn't say anything to her? When she
            came here?

AUDREY   Like what?

ZARA   To break us up.

AUDREY   Sweetheart. If you really loved each other, what
            could I say?

ZARA   Cos if you did, if you did say something, then
            you took away my life. My future. You realise
            that? So?

            Beat.

AUDREY   You'll have a wonderful future. Just wait and see.

            ZARA *looks at her.*

            CHERYL *and* MATTHEW *enter.* MATTHEW*'s
            carrying a spade.*

MATTHEW   We found it. Mrs Walters! We found it.

AUDREY   Matthew!

CHERYL   Oh. It's so sad.

MATTHEW   Propped up by the summerhouse.

CHERYL   Told him you were moving and he wouldn't shut
            up about his blessed spade, so I said let's go
            down and find it. Chance to see the place before
            the end. Well – not the end really, I suppose.
            A new owner.

ZARA   A developer. They're going to convert it to flats,
            and divide up the garden so each flat has
            a small patch of its own. It's good in a way.
            A natural extension. Democracy. More housing.

CHERYL   Flats?

ZARA   Yes.

CHERYL   Did no one want it all?

AUDREY   Not for a reasonable price.

CHERYL   How many people will live here?

ZARA   Thirty?

CHERYL   But oh, it's so sad. Mrs Walters. After what you
            wanted to do.

AUDREY   Yes well…

            It's not enough to have a dream, it turns out.
            When the house you remembered requires
            hundreds of thousands of pounds of work, just to
            stay up. And the garden even more. Ground
            water. Disease in half the trees. Miner bees
            everywhere. Ants. There's some things you can't
            restore. The earth itself. You know that Matthew.

MATTHEW   What?

AUDREY   And it's probably right that I refocus my efforts
            on the business. It's been suffering and we need
            to stabilise that. Build everything back up.
            Paul's right.

            She looks at them.

            The wrong thing, at the wrong time.

MATTHEW   Not been put to bed properly. Is Gabriel
            around?

ZARA   Not yet. He said he'd try to stop by.

CHERYL   We'll miss him then.

AUDREY   How are you?

CHERYL   Looking after each other. Aren't we?

MATTHEW   We are.

CHERYL   We have good sex.

            That's one of the points where we communicate
            exactly as we always did. It's good isn't it?

MATTHEW   I'm not sure I want to talk about that in front of –

CHERYL   What does it matter?

MATTHEW   I suppose not. Yes, we have very good sex
                Mrs Walters.

AUDREY   Well that's nice.

                Beat.

MATTHEW   Is Gabriel around?

CHERYL   Maybe later.

MATTHEW   So we'll miss him?

CHERYL   I think so. We should get back.

MATTHEW   Not much garden to see.

AUDREY   When it was confirmed, the sale, there didn't
                seem any point in expending any more time or
                money, so the whole thing will just...

MATTHEW   Rot.

AUDREY   Yes. Back into the ground.

                A long moment.

CHERYL   Shithole.

                Beat.

AUDREY   What will they look like? I can't imagine. What
                will they do to it? New cottages in the garden.
                Access roads.

ZARA   Homes. Which we need.

AUDREY   But who would live here if it's not beautiful?
                What would be the point?

ZARA   A roof over your head.

AUDREY   Is that it?

                A moment. AUDREY *reaches into her bag, and
                pulls out an envelope.*

                Cheryl I meant to give you something. I was
                going to post it. It's not a huge amount but just
                a way of saying thank you.

CHERYL   Oh. Well. We didn't expect.

AUDREY   It's not a huge amount.

              CHERYL opens it and looks.

CHERYL   It… Oh. No. Well… Anyway. It's appreciated.
              Thank you. Come on. We should get home.

MATTHEW   There should be roses. Here. And snowdrops.

CHERYL   Not at this time of year.

MATTHEW   March.

CHERYL   It's November.

MATTHEW   Smells like March.

              They head off.

AUDREY   Take care.

              They go.

              They won't be cheap. These flats. Don't think
              they'll go to some impoverished hard-working
              local couple. It'll be buy-to-lets and holidays
              mostly.

              A moment.

              Even with death most things carry on. Plants
              seed, children are born. Inheritance. One
              generation after another. But there is a time
              when that stops. When for one reason or
              another a species dies. A culture expires. That
              particular line of history comes to an end.

              I know you, and your friends, and Katherine,
              you all laughed at me for wanting to do this, but
              don't you think there was something, in all this,
              that was worth preserving? That some part of it,
              just some little part of it, might be *good*?

ZARA   You wanted it to be what you remembered –

AUDREY   This wasn't about me, really, Zara, it was so the
              world you, and your children were going to live

in had some sense of its past, its roots. So you weren't just living in the next email. The next… trend.

ZARA   I don't think I'll have children.

AUDREY looks at her.

GABRIEL enters. Holding a baby carrier.

GABRIEL   Hi.

AUDREY   Gabriel. Oh… You…

GABRIEL   He's asleep. Anna's just coming.

AUDREY   Anna?

GABRIEL   Yes.

AUDREY   I wrote and told her we were leaving, but I didn't hear back.

They gather round the baby.

ZARA   Isn't he beautiful?

AUDREY   Stanley.

ANNA enters.

ANNA   I braced myself for a change, but I had no idea. Hello.

AUDREY   Anna.

She goes to her. Kisses her, slightly awkwardly. ANNA lets her.

I didn't think you'd come.

ANNA   Are they literally about to arrive?

AUDREY   Yes, could be this afternoon apparently. They won't waste time.

AUDREY looks at the baby.

He looks like Zara. Your eyes though.

ANNA   He frowns sometimes. That's the one time I can see James in him.

A moment where they look at the baby.

AUDREY   You're staying?

ANNA   With Gabriel. For tonight.

AUDREY   And then?

ANNA   I'm renting a small cottage in the village.
My stuff arrives tomorrow morning.

AUDREY   You're going to… live here?

ANNA   Got more friends here than there.

AUDREY   …your flat in London?

ANNA   Not with Stanley. It's by a main road. We're
going to settle here. Save up. Then maybe, buy
one of these. When they've finished them.

AUDREY   You… Sweetheart, he's gone. Just ashes.

ANNA   Then why did it mean so much to you?

AUDREY   I wanted him to be at home.

ANNA   So why are you leaving?

Actually I know. What you think they say
about you after you leave the shop. Why no
one will return your calls. Why everybody gets
the newsletter through their door and you
don't. It's exactly what you think it is.

A moment. AUDREY *looks distraught.*

Someone has to do something, or it'll just be
some stranger living here. Trampling him with
no idea.

I'm going to find out which flat gets this bit of
garden, and I'll buy it and I'll live here with
Stanley.

AUDREY   You have to understand –

ANNA   You didn't know James by the way. The way
you talk about him. It's a different person to the
one I fell in love with.

AUDREY   Why would you say that? Now?

ANNA   Because you need to know –

AUDREY   I knew every part of him. He was my *son*. You
           were with him three months.

           You don't understand why he joined the army.
           Why he went to fight for the country, for the
           place he loved. If that confuses you then you
           didn't understand him at all. He *adored* this
           country and believed in it, and he –

ANNA   He didn't believe in it. What we were doing.
           Over there. He told me, he'd lost all hope it will
           ever get better. No strategy he said. Never had
           been. He thought it was a folly. He died for
           nothing.

AUDREY   Rubbish.

ZARA   Anna leave her alone –

ANNA   And then you scattered him in this mess. In this
           indulgent, waste of time.

           You ruined his life. Now you've ruined his
           death too.

           A moment.

AUDREY   I think even though this has failed, and we've
           had to give it up, there will be some value in
           what we achieved.

ANNA   What value?

AUDREY   Romance isn't false. It's spirit that can inspire
           real change.

ANNA   I don't know what that means.

AUDREY   Then *think about it*!

           The baby starts crying.

           Oh…

           ANNA *goes and rocks the baby carrier.*
           Soothes STANLEY.

ANNA	Alright. Alright…
AUDREY	Sorry…

Beat. GABRIEL *stands to one side, rolling a cigarette.*

ANNA	You going back to London too?
ZARA	Yes. Work.
ANNA	You mean writing?
ZARA	Yes…
ANNA	How's it going?
ZARA	My first novella is being read. So we'll see.

Beat.

How's yours?

GABRIEL	Sorry?
ZARA	How's your course? Did you do English in the end? Or creative writing?
GABRIEL	No… I… No.
ANNA	He didn't go. He has to look after his mum and the idea of them both surviving on the student loan, and then to come out with that amount of debt. It put him off.
GABRIEL	Maybe next year.
ANNA	He's working in Costa.

But still writing, when you can, aren't you?

GABRIEL *doesn't say anything.*

It's brilliant. It really is. Have you read it?

ZARA	I'd love to.
ANNA	But you haven't?
ZARA	I could put it in front of someone.

GABRIEL   You offered that before. I sent it to you.

Didn't hear back.

ZARA *looks at him.*

GABRIEL *lights the cigarette.*

PAUL *appears from round the side of the house, breezy.*

PAUL   Right! Half-twelve. Time to go. Anna! Gabriel.

GABRIEL   Hi.

PAUL   Hello!

ANNA *picks up the baby carrier.*

ANNA   I'll let you know where I end up.

AUDREY   You're welcome at ours. To stay. If you need to. For any reason. Do you want our new address? Paul can you –

ANNA   No thank you.

She goes, with the baby carrier.

GABRIEL *stands for a moment. Smoking.*

GABRIEL   I knew I'd see you today, and I knew you'd ask. I couldn't bear it. So I deleted it on my computer, then I took the originals, the notes, everything, put it in a pile in the garden and burned it.

Waste of time.

ZARA   I really hope it works out for you.

GABRIEL   I'll make coffee. Then I'll manage people making coffee. That'll be it.

He finishes the cigarette, throws it to the ground, stamps it out and leaves.

PAUL, ZARA *and* AUDREY *stand for a moment. An engine starts up nearby – revving.*

PAUL   I want you to know that I love you. Both of you.

                Always, and without question.

                Wherever we are. Whatever happens. I'll be
                with you.

                A moment.

ZARA   Thanks Paul.

PAUL   Alright then?

AUDREY   I want to stop this. I want to stay.

PAUL   I'm sorry?

AUDREY   I'm not selling the house. I'm going to stay
                living here.

PAUL   But Audrey, you can't.

AUDREY   Yes just stop them completing. We'll pay a fine
                but –

PAUL   We'll pay a huge fine.

ZARA   Mum come on it's all arranged.

AUDREY   It doesn't matter, we'll unarrange it. We haven't
                sold it yet.

PAUL   It'll ruin us. To stay here. You know how much
                we've lost. You know about the business. And
                we can't afford any of the work that needs doing.

AUDREY   I don't care. I'm staying. If you love me, you'll
                go and call them now and stop them. I'll do it
                myself if I need to. I'm not moving. I will fix it
                all piece by piece, inch by inch of this garden,
                I'll do it myself, with my hands. Finish the job.

                PAUL *looks at her.*

PAUL   You're serious.

AUDREY   Yes. It's up to you. Go back to London or stay
                with me, but I'm going to be here. I'm always
                going to be here.

                He looks at her. A moment.

PAUL   I better make some calls.

               He goes.

ZARA   Mum this is a mistake. He's right. You'll lose
               everything.

AUDREY   This is everything. Myself. My family. James.
               My past. My future. I don't want anything else
               but this piece of land.

               Make some tea.

               ZARA stares at her. Then goes.

               AUDREY's left alone on stage.

               She picks up the trowel PAUL gave her.

               *Sinks to her knees by one of the beds, and starts
               digging. Trying to put one of the plants, back
               upright and in the right place.*

               *She doesn't know what she's doing, but her
               hands and knees get muddy.*

               Then MATTHEW comes back on stage.

MATTHEW   A rose. They can't start work till we've
               transplanted the rose. Do they know about the
               rose? Very rare. Mrs Walters! Tell them to stop.
               There's a rose. It survived the war. We have to
               keep it!

               The sound of a baby crying.

               The stage darkens.

               *The last pieces of the garden rot even more.
               The ground is returned to soil. The house is
               destroyed.*

               Darkness. Soil. A battlefield.

               *From out of the darkness appears STANLEY,
               dressed in slightly futuristic body armour,
               holding a gun.*

               AUDREY turns and looks at him.

               End of play.

www.nickhernbooks.co.uk

facebook.com/nickhernbooks

twitter.com/nickhernbooks